go
for
it!

FREDDY, FORK IT OVER!

‖ I0133055

✱✱✱✱✱✱✱✱✱✱✱✱✱✱✱✱✱✱✱✱✱✱✱✱✱✱✱✱✱✱✱✱
Dedicated to all those whose imaginations open up a new world of possibilities
✱✱✱✱✱✱✱✱✱✱✱✱✱✱✱✱✱✱✱✱✱✱✱✱✱✱✱✱✱✱✱✱

Farah Salim Eck
Brandy Moore Grove

My Favorite Recipes!

Write your favorite recipes and the page numbers on the sticky notes below so that you can find them easily and make them often with your family!

Recipe #1

Page #

Recipe #2

Page #

Recipe #3

Page #

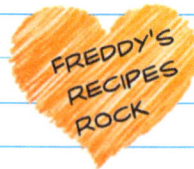
FREDDY'S RECIPES ROCK

Ingredients for Success

Freddy, Fork it Over! is a project that took many years and many people to complete. But this labor of love was so important to develop as a way to help kids learn how to make better choices. In all aspects of life, there are certain ingredients for success, and together we created a notebook that hopefully provides each and every reader with some of those ingredients like:
- Hard work & learning from mistakes
- Willpower, dedication & wanting to improve yourself each day
- Ability to appreciate differences & to try new things

Many, many thanks go to our volunteer professionals who offered their services:
 ★Tina Lieberman, Black Willow Photography - Recipe Photos
 ★Miranda Singler, Freelance Illustrator and Graphic Artist - Illustrations
 ★Connie Dilley, Kimberly Eck, Lou Ann Moore, Barbara Rowe, Barbara Salim, Merle Shiffman, and Julie Waldrop - Editors

Freddy, Fork it Over! is the result of a lot of hard work and many ingredients for success: Brandy's tireless efforts to make delicious and nutritious recipes that kids would love; Farah's creative touch designing the notebook and creating fun activities; combined with the talents and help of many other taste testers, recipe makers, editors, and volunteers. Every recipe has been tested and approved by a panel of parents and kids, so you're sure to find some new dishes you love along with twists on old favorites!

We hope you enjoy cooking and learning from Freddy and the Silverton family as much as we enjoyed creating Freddy, Fork it Over!

Brandy Moore Grove

THANK YOU!

Farah Salim Eck

Table of Contents

SAFE COOKING TEMPERATURES
as measured with a food thermometer

Meat & Meat Mixtures — Internal temperature
Beef, Pork, Veal, Lamb _____ 160°F
Turkey, Chicken _____ 165°F

Beef, Pork, Veal & Lamb _____ 145°F
with a 3 minute rest time

Poultry
Chicken & Turkey, Whole _____ 165°F
Poultry Parts _____ 165°F
Duck & Goose _____ 165°F
Stuffing (cooked alone or in bird) _____ 165°F

Ham
Fresh (raw) _____ 160°F
Pre-cooked (to reheat) _____ 140°F

Eggs & Egg Dishes
Eggs _____ Cook until yolk & white are firm
Egg Dishes _____ 160°F

Seafood
Fin Fish _____ 145°F
or flesh is opaque and separates easily with fork
Shrimp, Lobster & Crabs _____ Flesh pearly & opaque
Clams, Oysters & Mussels _____ Shells open during cooking
Scallops _____ Milky white or opaque & firm

How to Use This Guide

The Level indicates whether the recipe is one, two or three stars (see page 3)

Name of the recipe is written at the top left

The list of ingredients is always on the left side of the photo

Page numbers are in the upper right corner

The computer printout shows the nutritional content for one serving. Check out the "Know Your Nutritional Numbers" on page 4 to help you be mindful of your calories, fat, sugars, and sodium so that you make healthy choices!

The colors of the Recipe card show which type of food or meal it is:
- Yellow - Breakfast
- Orange - Lunch
- Dinner - Blue
- Purple - Party Treats/Snacks

YUM!

Recipe Card (example)

Sugar & Spice Popcorn

Level - ★

page 11

ingredients
3 cups of plain microwave popcorn (popped)
2 tablespoons sugar
6-8 sprays canola oil non stick cooking spray
½ teaspoon cinnamon
¼ teaspoon nutmeg

The oldest popcorn ever found was discovered in the "Bat Cave" located in New Mexico.

Nutrition Content for One Serving:

Calories	Fat	Saturated Fat	Carbohydrates	Sodium	Sugars
27	2 g	<1 g	4 g	45 mg	<1 g

RECIPE

Prepare popcorn according to package instructions.

Place hot popcorn in large bowl and spray with non stick cooking spray. Add sugar and spices.

Toss gently until everything is mixed well.

Makes four servings.

Did You Know?
Popcorn is one of the oldest snacks - Native American Indians popped corn over campfires almost 5,000 years ago! Popcorn is thought to have originally come from Mexico, but is now eaten all around the world!

Meet the Silvertons

We, the Silvertons, are just like any other family: we like to get together for holidays, play games, and do activities as a group. The only difference is we are a family of silverware, just like the kind that you use to eat!

Freddy Silverton is a very curious and intelligent young fork who will travel with you throughout this guide to help you to understand certain terms and ways to eat and exercise to be healthy.

Other Silverton family members, including Mama Spoon, Father Knife, Baby Spoon, Grandma Whisk, Grandpa Ladle, Uncle Tongs, Cousin Grater, Aunt Spatula, and so many more of their friends and relatives have added their tips, suggestions, and fun activities throughout this guide.

We hope this guide will help you discover how fun it can be to learn about nutrition and delicious food you can make yourself. You'll also be able to get some new ideas and ways to stay healthy through exercise and making good food choices. So grab your own Silverton family utensils and explore this notebook to become fitter and healthier by the forkful!

Bon Appetit!

UNCLE TONGS   Father Knife   Aunt Spatula

Grandma Whisk   FREDDY FORK   Grandpa Ladle

Baby Spoon   Mama Spoon   Cousin Grater

Silverton Star Levels ⭐ / ⭐⭐ / ⭐⭐⭐

Each recipe is marked with either one, two, or three stars. The stars indicate the appropriate age level for kids to do certain things in the kitchen with or without adult supervision and help. Please follow the star levels so that you don't get hurt.

Ages 6-8 (⭐): Constant supervision for all activities in the kitchen

- Measuring, pouring, mixing, or stirring
- Taking stems off food
- Washing fruits and veggies
- Putting ingredients into blender
- Tearing lettuce for salads
- NO cutting or working with any heat
- Knead bread dough, cut cookies with a cookie cutter

Ages 8-10 (⭐⭐) Need supervision but can do some activities on own

(all of the above, plus:)
- Can use oven and other heating elements with supervision
- Cracking eggs
- Coating meats with dry rubs and marinades
- Making basic pastries
- Beating with a hand-held electric mixer
- Fix own sandwiches

Ages 10 and above (⭐⭐⭐)

(all of the above, plus:)
This is the age that most kids can start cooking simple meals on their own. They will still need some supervision when using sharp knives, if they are anywhere near open flames, and/or if the recipe is difficult or complicated.

Know Your Nutritional Numbers

The recipes in this guide were created using the Daily Nutritional Guidelines for Children as a reference. A chart is included with each recipe to show the nutritional information based on one serving size. Below is a chart that outlines the daily nutritional recommendations for kids of different ages, and sometimes by gender (girl or boy).

Daily Nutritional Guidelines for Children Between Age 4-13

Nutrients	4-8 years old	9-13 years old
Calories	1,400 - 1,600	1,600 - 2,000 (girls) / 1,800 - 2,200 (boys)
Fat	39 g - 62 g	62 g - 85 g
Saturated Fat	16 g - 18 g	18 g - 22 g (girls) / 20 g - 24 g (boys)
Sodium	1,200 mg - 1,900 mg	1,500 mg - 2,200 mg

Kids who are very active (more than 1 hour per day, 6 days per week) may need more daily calories, while kids who are less active will need to eat fewer calories.

Don't eat more than 12 grams or 3 teaspoons of added sugar per day

This is a sample nutrition label found on lots of food items:

Start here to see how big the servings are →

Be sure to understand how many calories are in a serving

Limit these nutrients (make sure they aren't too high or it's not a healthy choice)

Get enough of these nutrients (they should be high numbers)

Generally, 5% or less is low and 20% or more is high for one meal or snack

Nutrition Facts

Serving Size 1 slice (47 g)
Servings Per Container 6

Amount Per Serving

Calories 100   **Calories from Fat** 90

	% Daily Value
Total Fat 10 g	15%
Saturated Fat 2.5 g	11%
Trans Fat 2 g	
Cholesterol 0 mg	0%
Sodium 300 mg	12%
Total Carb 15 g	5%
Dietary Fiber < 1 g	3%
Sugars 1 g	
Protein 3 g	

Vitamin A 0%	Vitamin C 4%
Calcium 45 %	Iron 6%
Thiamin 8%	Riboflavin 6%
Niacin 6%	

*Percent Daily Values are based on a 2,000 calorie diet. Your daily values may be higher or lower depending on your calorie needs.

Adapted from the American Heart Association

Breakfast

Breakfast Recipes:

Portion Sizes Cheat Sheet
(for one meal)

Protein — each meal, eat the size of a → **deck of playing cards**

BEEF

Vegetables — each meal, eat the size of a → **baseball**

Grains — each meal, eat the size of a → **CD case**

SPAGHETTI   WHOLE WHEAT

Fruits — each meal, eat the size of a → **tennis ball**

Huevos Rancheros

Level = ★★★

ingredients:

4 corn tortillas
4 large eggs
1 cup salsa (see page 46 for recipe)
2 tablespoons fat-free cheddar cheese (shredded)
1 teaspoon sea salt
¼ teaspoon ground black pepper

Eggs are Egg-celent sources of protein!

Huevos Rancheros means "Ranch Eggs" in Spanish.

Instructions:

(1) Heat flat square skillet or a small round skillet to medium heat. Spray tortillas on both sides with non-stick cooking spray and add pinch of sea salt. Depending on size of skillet, place 1 or 2 tortillas on skillet when warm. When one side is crunchy and slightly browned, turn over and cook until crunchy and slightly browned on other side. Place tortillas on individual plates.

(2) Next, depending on size of skillet you are using, crack one egg at a time (if using small skillet cook one egg at a time; if using larger skillet cook more than one egg at a time but keep eggs from touching). Put a pinch of sea salt and pepper on each egg.

(3) Cook egg on medium heat until firm and solid on one side, and flip to cook other side. Add pinch of salt and pepper on other side before it finishes cooking.

(4) Place one egg on each tortilla. In a small saucepan, heat salsa over medium heat until bubbly.

(5) Spoon ¼ cup of warmed salsa and shredded cheese on each egg. Makes 4 servings.

Nutrition Content for One Serving:

Calories	Fat	Saturated Fat	Carbohydrates	Sodium	Sugars
86	4 g	2 g	8 g	495 mg	2 g

Strawberry Shortcake Smoothie

Level = ⭐

ingredients:

1 16-ounce container fat-free plain yogurt
1 banana (sliced)
1 cup of ice cubes
¾ cup 100% pure orange juice (pulp optional)
2 tablespoons wheat germ
1 10-ounce package frozen strawberries (partially thawed)

Shortcake is made from dough that's "short" because it bakes with a lot of crumbly texture.

Nutrition Content for One Smoothie:

Calories	Fat	Saturated Fat	Carbohydrates	Sodium	Sugars
165	<1 g	<1 g	37 g	73 mg	24 g

RECIPE

Place all ingredients in a blender. Blend for 30 seconds-1 minute or until smooth. You may need to add a ¼ cup more orange juice and blend again for better consistency (thickness).

Pour into glass. Add a fresh strawberry as shown in the photo for a delicious garnish!

Makes 4 servings.

Cream de la Crepe

Level = ★★

Cream ingredients:

6 tablespoons fat-free cream cheese
8-ounce container fat-free plain yogurt
½ teaspoon lemon juice
1 cup strawberries (fresh or frozen, sliced, thawed, stems removed)
¼ teaspoon ground cinnamon
1 cup peaches (fresh or frozen, sliced, and peeled)
1 teaspoon sugar

Crepe ingredients:

2 eggs
¾ cup skim milk
½ cup water
1 cup all-purpose flour
2 tablespoons wheat germ
1 teaspoon real vanilla extract
2 ½ tablespoons sugar
3 tablespoons unsalted butter

YOGURT

Baby Spoon's Tip

If the batter is too thick, add 1 tablespoon of water to thin it out.

TIP

Crepes are French pancakes that are filled and rolled up!

Recipe Instructions:

Place all crepe ingredients in blender, pulse for 10 seconds. Scrape sides and pulse again for a few seconds. Put batter into a container, cover, and refrigerate for 1 hour. Spray a skillet with non-stick cooking spray and set to medium heat. When pan is hot, pour in ¼ cup batter. Lift and rotate pan to swirl batter around until it begins to cook and firm up. Cook each crepe for 30-60 seconds, then flip it over and cook until golden brown. Remove crepes from skillet and place on plate until all are finished cooking.

In medium bowl, use electric mixer to blend yogurt and cream cheese. When smooth, add lemon juice and mix well. In another bowl add sugar to strawberries and peaches. Add 1 ½ tablespoons of yogurt mixture and 2 tablespoons of fruit mixture in center of crepe and sprinkle with cinnamon. Roll each crepe, place seam side down on a plate and top with yogurt and fruit mixture. Makes 4-6 servings.

Nutrition Content for One Serving:

Calories	Fat	Saturated Fat	Carbohydrates	Sodium	Sugars
204	6 g	4 g	27 g	144 mg	10 g

Skinny Mini Muffin Top

Level = ★★

ingredients:

1 whole wheat English muffin

1 tablespoon fat-free vegetable OR chive-flavored cream cheese

½ cup cucumber (thinly sliced)

½ cup tomato (finely chopped) OR ½ cup sun-dried tomatoes (finely chopped) packed in olive oil

¼ teaspoon dried basil

2 slices fat-free cheese such as Swiss, Provolone, White Cheddar, Monterey Jack, or Havarti

OPTIONAL: 1 Portobello mushroom or 4 button mushrooms (thinly sliced)

OPTIONAL: ⅛ teaspoon dried dill

Sea salt and ground black pepper to taste

English muffins are called that everywhere outside of England, but in England they're just called muffins!

Nutrition Content for One Muffin:

Calories	Fat	Saturated Fat	Carbohydrates	Sodium	Sugars
163	6 g	3 g	19 g	267 mg	4 g

RECIPE

Cut muffin in half and toast both sides in a toaster.

Spread cream cheese on each half of muffin. Top each muffin half with cucumber, tomato, mushroom, basil, dill, salt, pepper, and a slice of cheese. Microwave on high 1 minute or until cheese is melted.

Makes 2 servings.

Banana Splits Waffles

Level = ★★★

Waffle Ingredients:

¾ cup all-purpose flour
½ cup whole wheat flour
2 teaspoons baking powder
½ teaspoon salt
2 tablespoons sugar
2 eggs (separated)
1 cup skim milk
6 tablespoons unsalted butter (melted & cooled)

Nutrition Content for One Serving:

Calories	Fat	Saturated Fat	Carbohydrates	Sodium	Sugars
239	10 g	7 g	35 g	290 mg	15 g

Topping Ingredients:

3 large ripe bananas
½ tablespoon unsalted butter
3 tablespoons light brown sugar
¼ cup 100% pure orange juice (no pulp)
⅛ teaspoon ground cinnamon

Waffle Instructions:

Mix the flours, baking powder, salt, and sugar together in a bowl. In a separate bowl, whisk egg yolks, milk, and melted butter together with a fork, then stir this mixture into dry ingredients to make a smooth batter. In a clean bowl, use electric mixer or whisk to beat eggs whites until stiff peaks form. Fold into batter mixture. Spoon 2 large tablespoons of batter into a preheated waffle maker and cook until waffle is golden brown.

Topping Instructions:

Cut bananas in slices. Melt butter in a non-stick skillet over medium-high heat. Add brown sugar, then lay banana slices on top. Cook for 20 seconds, add orange juice and cinnamon. Cook for 10 more seconds, then turn bananas carefully and cook for 45-60 seconds more, covering with pan sauce. Divide banana slices between waffles.
Makes 6-8 waffles.

Biscuit Bites

Level = ★★

ingredients:

1 cup whole wheat flour
1 cup all-purpose flour
1 tablespoon baking powder
1/2 teaspoon baking soda
2 teaspoons sugar
1/2 teaspoon salt
1 cup non-fat buttermilk (cold)
1 stick unsalted butter (cold and cut into pieces)

What do you use to put on top of your biscuits? Jam, gravy, butter, syrup...? All of them?!

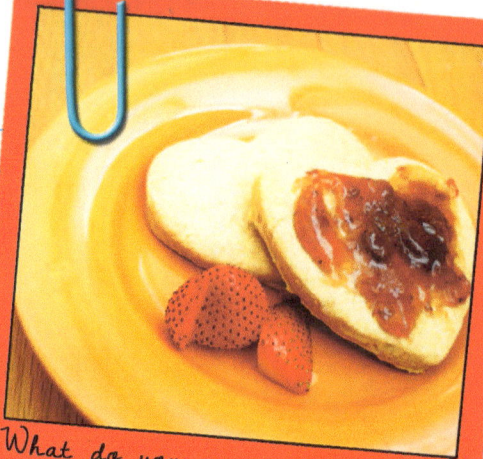

CULTURAL BITES
In America, biscuits are bread-like baked goods, while in England, biscuits are sweet baked goods, similar to what Americans call cookies!

Nutrition Content for One Biscuit:

Calories	Fat	Saturated Fat	Carbohydrates	Sodium	Sugars
130	6 g	1 g	16 g	479 mg	2 g

RECIPE

Preheat oven to 450°F.

In a large bowl whisk both types of flour, baking powder, baking soda, sugar, and salt. Cut in butter until mixture is grainy and coarse. Add buttermilk to dry ingredients, stirring until they're moistened. Turn dough out onto a lightly floured surface and knead lightly 4-5 times. Roll or pat dough out to about 1-inch thickness. Cut with large cookie cutters to make fun shapes and place on ungreased baking sheet. Bake for 12-14 minutes or until golden brown.

Serve with optional sugar-free preserves or honey, or make a breakfast sandwich. Makes about 12 biscuits.

Variations:
You can add additional ingredients after the butter is added. For sweet biscuits, add 2 more teaspoons sugar & 1/2 teaspoon cinnamon. For savory biscuits, add 1/2 teaspoon dried chives, 1/2 cup any variety fat-free shredded cheese, & a 1/2 cup sun-dried tomatoes packed in olive oil, drained & finely chopped.

Fruit Drop Dish

Level = ✹✹

ingredients:

2 cups quick cooking oats
½ cup packed brown sugar
⅓ cup raisins
⅓ cup dried cherries
⅓ cup dried apricots (chopped)
1 tablespoon walnuts (chopped)
½ teaspoon ground cinnamon
1 teaspoon baking powder
2 tablespoons unsalted butter
½ cup unsweetened applesauce
1½ cups skim milk
1 large egg (beaten)

Ancient Romans called walnuts "Jupiter's Royal Acorns."

Even people in the Stone Ages knew that breakfast was the most important meal of the day! Cavemen used stones to grind grains they found to make a kind of porridge to eat in the morning.

RECIPE

Preheat oven to 375°F.

Combine first 8 ingredients in a medium bowl.
Combine milk, applesauce, butter, and egg.
Add milk mixture to oat mixture; stir well.
Pour oat mixture into 8-inch square baking dish coated with non-stick cooking spray. Bake for 20 minutes.

Serve while it's warm.

Makes 6 servings.

Nutrition Content for One Serving:

Calories	Fat	Saturated Fat	Carbohydrates	Sodium	Sugars
307	6 g	1 g	58 g	166 mg	37 g

Cookie Cutter Omelets
Level = ★★★

ingredients:

8 large eggs
$\frac{1}{2}$ cup mushrooms (chopped)
$\frac{1}{2}$ cup yellow onion (chopped)
$\frac{1}{2}$ cup green bell pepper (chopped)
$\frac{1}{2}$ cup tomato (chopped, seeds removed)
$\frac{1}{4}$ cup fat-free sharp cheddar cheese (shredded)
$\frac{1}{2}$ teaspoon dried dill
$\frac{1}{2}$ teaspoon salt
$\frac{1}{4}$ teaspoon ground black pepper
$\frac{3}{4}$ cup fresh spinach (shredded)

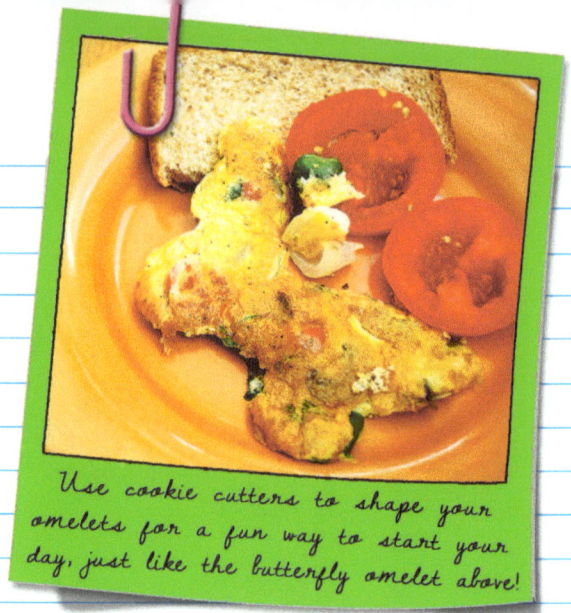

Use cookie cutters to shape your omelets for a fun way to start your day, just like the butterfly omelet above!

RECIPE

Place all ingredients in large mixing bowl and whisk together. Spray large skillet with non-stick cooking spray and place burner on medium heat.

Pour egg mixture into skillet and cook over medium heat until egg begins to set on one side. Flip and cook other side until set. It could take 4-8 minutes to cook, depending on size of skillet.

Remove omelet from skillet and put on large plate or cutting board. Use cookie cutters to cut shapes out of omelet.

Serve with whole wheat toast. Makes 6-8 omelets depending on size of cookie cutters and skillet.

Eggs-celent Spin

You can tell if an egg is raw or hard-boiled just by spinning it! Because the liquids have set into a solid, a hard-boiled egg will easily spin. But if you feel or hear moving liquid in the egg when it spins, it's raw!

Nutrition Content for One Omelet:

Calories	Fat	Saturated Fat	Carbohydrates	Sodium	Sugars
94	6 g	2 g	3 g	239 mg	1 g

Breakfast Burger

Level = ★★★

ingredients:

1 pound lean ground turkey
1 large egg (lightly beaten)
1/4 teaspoon ground sage
1/4 teaspoon dried parsley
1/4 teaspoon ground black pepper
1/4 teaspoon ground allspice
1 medium Bosc pear (peeled, cored, and coarsely grated)
OR 1 15-ounce canned pear halves in 100% fruit juice (drained and diced)
3/4 teaspoon salt

Pear-ry weird! Pears are part of the rose flower family.

TIP:
If the mixture is not thick enough, ground 1-2 slices of whole grain bread into crumbs and add to mixture.

Patties can be formed (but not cooked) up to 3 hours ahead and chilled (cover with plastic wrap).

RECIPE

Stir together all ingredients in a large bowl until combined well. With moistened hands, form mixture into patties using approximately 1/4 cup per patty (about 3 inches in diameter or about 8 total). Arrange on a tray lined with wax paper.

Lightly brush a 12-inch nonstick skillet with oil. Heat skillet over moderate heat until hot but not smoking. Cook patties in batches of 4, turning over once, until browned and cooked (about 6 minutes per batch).

Makes about 8 patties.

Nutrition Content for One Burger:

Calories	Fat	Saturated Fat	Carbohydrates	Sodium	Sugars
132	8 g	2 g	4 g	363 mg	4 g

Pantastic Pancakes
Level = ★★

ingredients:

2 eggs
1 ¼ cups skim milk
3 tablespoons unsalted butter
1 teaspoon real vanilla extract
¾ cups all-purpose flour
¾ cups whole wheat flour
¾ teaspoon salt
2 teaspoons baking powder
½ cup fresh blueberries
1 ripe banana (mashed)
1 tablespoon sugar

Even William Shakespeare must have loved pancakes - he mentioned them in several of his plays!

Nutrition Content for One Pancake:

Calories	Fat	Saturated Fat	Carbohydrates	Sodium	Sugars
155	5 g	3 g	24 g	367 mg	6 g

RECIPE

Melt butter in a small saucepan on low heat and set aside to cool. Mix eggs, milk, butter, and vanilla in medium bowl with a whisk until well blended.

Mix all dry ingredients together in a large bowl. Gently fold in egg mixture, banana, and blueberries and quickly stir until completely mixed. Let batter rest while griddle is heating to medium heat (batter will thicken upon standing). Spray preheated griddle with non-stick cooking spray and pour ¼ cup of batter on griddle.

Cook on one side until bubbles begin to form. Then turn pancakes and cook on other side until brown. Makes about 8 pancakes.

Lunch Recipes:

Can you find the different kind of sandwich toppings in the word search below? Look diagonally, vertically, and horizontally.

```
U Q Y I I Z D N D E I Z Y A T
S T R V T E A R A C Q H L O W
T O M A T O O F A U Y V M E Z
O R E B M U C U C T F W R X Z
V N W O F K A I B T S L L M X
G K I D I P T G P E I U A N L
A H W O N K I J O L B Y M O B
W C U C N S G S J T O P D R G
X A Y C U S L R H N L N S T R
V R M X C G V P N S I J Z X S
X B A S C C H A A D V L J A X
C P U E Q Y I B W F E P I Q Q
M E Q E P S S B S B S R Z T R
D Y B S E E L Y J U J A X C T
W Q P O L Z W A X H F Q Q N J
W B G K T K S Y Y I U L L U L
P Z C R O A O R S K E N G W T
L I Z L Y B P G T I X I Y U T
P G W D T R Q W S H I M X V S
Q Y P X P M C R D T T L N P J
```

CUCUMBER   OLIVES

LETTUCE   ONIONS

MAYONNAISE   PICKLES

MUSTARD   TOMATO

Pizzaz Pizza Pita

Level = ★★

ingredients:

1 whole wheat pita

3 tablespoons no-salt-added tomato sauce

2 tablespoons green bell peppers (chopped)

2 tablespoons mushrooms (chopped)

2 tablespoons broccoli (chopped)

2 tablespoons onion (chopped)

$\frac{1}{4}$ teaspoon salt

3 tablespoons fat-free shredded mozzarella cheese

$\frac{1}{2}$ teaspoon garlic (minced)

$\frac{1}{4}$ teaspoon ground black pepper

$\frac{1}{4}$ teaspoon dried basil

$\frac{1}{4}$ teaspoon ground thyme

$\frac{1}{4}$ teaspoon dried oregano

other desired toppings

All mushrooms are fungi but not all fungi are mushrooms!

CULTURAL BITES

Favorite pizza toppings around the world:

- America: pepperoni
- India: pickled ginger
- Japan: eel and squid
- Brazil: green peas
- Russia: red herring

RECIPE

Add herbs, garlic, and salt to tomato sauce. Add $\frac{1}{2}$ teaspoon sugar for a sweeter sauce, or season with another pinch of salt, if desired. Spread sauce, toppings, and cheese on top of pita like you would a pizza (do not split pita open) and bake at 400°F until cheese is melted, or for about 10 minutes.

Makes 1 serving.

Other healthy toppings you might add:
- carrots (shredded)
- black olives (sliced)
- yellow bell peppers (diced)
- red bell peppers (diced)

Nutrition Content for One Pizza (prepared according to recipe):

Calories	Fat	Saturated Fat	Carbohydrates	Sodium	Sugars
210	2 g	<1 g	36 g	1172 mg	5 g

Moroccan Mix

Level = ★★

ingredients:

1 10-ounce box plain couscous
1 cucumber (diced)
1 pint grape tomatoes (cut in half)
3 carrots (diced)
1 bunch green onions (chopped)
1 cup fresh basil or mint
½ cup olive oil
2 tablespoons red wine vinegar
1 tablespoon sugar
½ teaspoon ground black pepper
½ teaspoon salt
juice squeezed from 1 lemon

Couscous originated in Morocco and is made from steamed grains of dough.

Couscous can be served as a type of cereal for breakfast, topped as a salad, or sweetened to serve as dessert.

RECIPE

Prepare couscous according to instructions on box. Add cucumber, tomatoes, carrots, green onions, and basil (or mint) to couscous and mix thoroughly. Combine olive oil, lemon juice, vinegar, sugar, salt, and pepper and shake well. Pour dressing over couscous and mix thoroughly.

Chill for at least 2 hours before serving.

Makes 8 servings.

Nutrition Content for One Serving:

Calories	Fat	Saturated Fat	Carbohydrates	Sodium	Sugars
135	10 g	1 g	12 g	170 mg	4 g

Souper Tomato Bowl

Level = ★★

ingredients:

½ tablespoon olive oil
2 teaspoons garlic (minced)
2 stalks green onion (chopped)
½ teaspoon sugar
¼ teaspoon sea salt (additional to taste)
1 cup no-salt-added tomato juice
½ cup skim milk
2 tablespoons fresh basil leaves (shredded) OR 1 teaspoon dried basil
2 large red tomatoes and 2 large yellow tomatoes (roughly chopped)
↳ OR 2 14.5 ounce cans no-salt-added diced tomatoes

The Super Bowl is measured in Roman numerals because a football season runs over 2 years.

KEY:
I (1)   II (2)   III (3)
IV (4)   V (5)
VI (6)   VII (7)
VIII (8)   IX (9)
X (10)

RECIPE

Heat olive oil in large soup or stew pot on medium to high heat. Add garlic and green onion. Saute until green onion is tender, about 1-2 minutes. Add sugar, salt, pepper, and dried basil if using; stir to incorporate. If using fresh basil, do not add it yet.

Add tomatoes, green pepper, and tomato juice. Stir to incorporate. Add milk. Bring to a boil for 8 minutes. Turn heat to low and add fresh basil if desired; simmer 1 to 2 minutes. Taste. Add more salt, pepper, herbs, and/or spices as desired.

Makes 4 servings.

Using the key above, can you figure out what the Roman numeral is below?

$$X + IV = ?$$

Answer: 14

Nutrition Content for One Serving:

Calories	Fat	Saturated Fat	Carbohydrates	Sodium	Sugars
58	<1 g	<1 g	11 g	177 mg	8 g

PBJ Quesadilla

Level = **

ingredients:

2 whole wheat tortillas
1 tablespoon sugar-free jelly
1 banana (peeled and sliced)
1 tablespoon reduced-fat natural peanut
   butter

In 1880 George Washington Carver discovered 300 uses for peanuts!

RECIPE

Place whole wheat tortilla on a plate. Spread peanut butter evenly over bottom tortilla. Place banana slices over peanut butter. Place second tortilla on top of bananas. Spray skillet with non-stick cooking spray and carefully place quesadilla in skillet to warm or place in a pre-heated quesadilla maker for 5 minutes.

Warm on one side (about 3-5 minutes), flip and warm on other side until both sides are crispy. Remove from pan or quesadilla maker and place on plate. Cut into slices like a pizza. Dunk quesadilla slices in jelly.

Makes 4 servings.

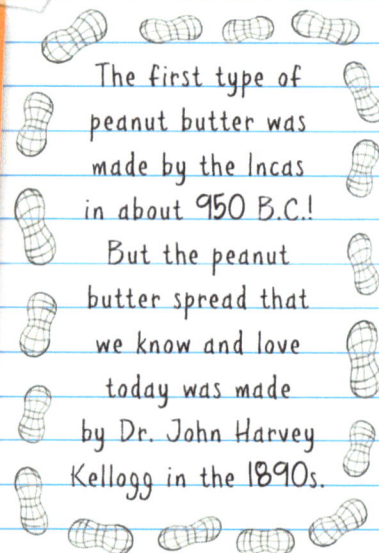

The first type of peanut butter was made by the Incas in about 950 B.C.! But the peanut butter spread that we know and love today was made by Dr. John Harvey Kellogg in the 1890s.

		Nutrition Content for One Slice:			
Calories	Fat	Saturated Fat	Carbohydrates	Sodium	Sugars
84	4 g	<1 g	16 g	158 mg	3 g

Grilled Tomatowich

page 23

Level = ✶✶

ingredients:

8 slices whole wheat bread
4 slices cheddar cheese
4 slices mozzarella cheese
4 slices deli ham
1 large tomato (cut into 8 slices)
4 slices roasted red peppers (from jar)
12 large leaves fresh basil

Even though tomatoes themselves are safe to eat, their leaves are toxic and unhealthy.

RECIPE

Dab red peppers with paper towel to dry. Coat both sides of bread with olive oil-flavored cooking spray. In large non-stick skillet over medium heat, cook bread on one side for 2 minutes, or until lightly toasted. Do this in batches, if necessary. Remove from pan.

Arrange 4 slices of bread on a work surface, toasted side up. Add ham, peppers, cheese, tomato, and basil to toasted slices. Top with remaining bread slices, with toasted side down.

Carefully place sandwiches in skillet. Cook for 2 minutes per side, or until toasted and cheese melts. Makes 4 sandwiches.

Nutrition Content for One Sandwich:

Calories	Fat	Saturated Fat	Carbohydrates	Sodium	Sugars
342	14 g	7 g	31 g	1319 mg	5 g

Hot Diggity Turkey Dog

Level = ★

ingredients:

1 100% turkey fat-free hot dog
1 8-inch whole wheat tortilla
1 tomato (sliced or ¼ cup chopped)
¼ cup lettuce (shredded)
2 tablespoons mild fat-free cheddar cheese (shredded)

Hot dogs are also called dogs, franks, frankfurters, weenies, wieners, and red hots!

Nutrition Content for One Wrap:

Calories	Fat	Saturated Fat	Carbohydrates	Sodium	Sugars
157	3 g	<1 g	27 g	863 mg	5 g

Eat at least 3 ounces of whole grain cereals, breads, crackers, rice or pasta every day. Whole grains list the following ingredients first on the label ingredient list: brown rice, bulgur, whole grain barley, graham flour, oatmeal, whole grain corn, whole oats, whole rye, whole wheat, or wild rice.

RECIPE

Using a fork, poke holes in turkey hot dog and microwave on high for 30-45 seconds. Slice hot dog in half lengthwise. Place hot dog in center of tortilla, cover hot dog with cheese. You can also add any sauce if you'd like. Place on microwave-safe plate and microwave on high for 10-15 seconds until cheese starts to melt.

Add shredded lettuce and 2 slices of tomato. Fold ends of tortilla in at each end of hot dog, then fold over tortilla and wrap around. Place the seam side down and it's ready to bite!

Makes 1 serving.

woof!

Ceviche Salad

Level = ★★

ingredients:

1 cup cucumbers (peeled and chopped)

½ cup green onion (chopped)

½ cup sliced radishes (cut in half)

1 pint cherry tomatoes (cut in half)

1 tablespoon extra virgin olive oil

1 teaspoon garlic (minced)

2 medium avocados (chopped)

1 large orange (seeded, peeled and cut into chunks)

5-ounce bag of veggie salad mix (with carrots and snow peas)

12 ounces fresh or thawed frozen large shrimp (peeled, deveined, tails removed, and cut in half)

½ teaspoon sea salt

¼ teaspoon ground black pepper

vinaigrette ingredients:

4 tablespoons 100% orange juice

½ teaspoon orange zest

1 tablespoon agave nectar

2 tablespoons white wine vinegar

2 tablespoons orange marmalade

¼ teaspoon sea salt

⅛ teaspoon ground black pepper

1 tablespoon extra virgin olive oil

¼ teaspoon dried tarragon

¼ teaspoon dried parsley

¼ teaspoon dried dill

¼ teaspoon dried basil

Ceviche is the Spanish word for seafood dishes which are usually marinated in citrus and spices.

RECIPE

Mix ingredients for vinaigrette in bowl with whisk. Add 1 tablespoon olive oil and minced garlic to skillet, and heat on medium for 1 minute. Season shrimp with salt and pepper, then place in one layer on bottom of hot skillet. Cook uncovered on medium heat for 8 minutes on one side. Flip each shrimp and cook on other side for about 4 minutes (until translucent, meaning you can see through them).

While shrimp are cooking, mix salad with vinaigrette. Divide salad mix into 4 bowls and layer cut fruits and veggies on top of salad – cucumber, green onion, tomato, radishes, and then oranges. Top each bowl with chopped avocado.

Drain shrimp on paper towel and add to each salad bowl. Makes 4 servings.

Nutrition Content for One Serving:

Calories	Fat	Saturated Fat	Carbohydrates	Sodium	Sugars
410	22 g	3 g	38 g	662 mg	15 g

Fiesta Wrap

Level = **

ingredients:

1 whole wheat tortilla

½ or whole grilled chicken breast
(size needed depends on how big tortilla is)

2 tablespoons taco sauce

2 tablespoons fat-free cheddar cheese (shredded)

¼ cup lettuce (shredded)

Fiesta means "party" or a "celebration" in Spanish.

RECIPE

Cook chicken breast on a stovetop grill or electric countertop grill. Cook until juices run clear or chicken is no longer pink in middle. You may have to slice chicken open in middle to check.

To determine doneness, chicken should reach 165°F using a kitchen thermometer. Once chicken is done, slice and place on tortilla. Add cheese.

Place wrap on a microwave-safe plate and microwave for 30-45 seconds or until cheese is melted. Add lettuce and sauce. Roll wrap into a bundle, and enjoy!

Makes 1 serving.

Measurement Mumble Jumble:

Can you finish the words below about measurement? Each blank needs a missing letter.

1. table_ _ _ _ _
2. measuring _ _ _
3. serv_ _ _
4. ha_f
5. _ _ _ spoon
6. qu_ _ t

Answers are below but don't peek until after you try!

Nutrition Content for One Serving:

Calories	Fat	Saturated Fat	Carbohydrates	Sodium	Sugars
241	4 g	<1 g	25 g	1067 mg	4 g

ANSWERS: 1. tablespoon 2. measuring cup 3. serving 4. half 5. teaspoon 6. quart

Mind Your Peas & Q's Salad

Level = ✹✹

ingredients:

5 asparagus spears (chopped)
3 garlic cloves (minced)
2 green onions (thinly sliced)
1 or 2 medium carrots (chopped)
1 red bell pepper (chopped)
1 large tomato (chopped)
1 15-ounce can white beans (rinsed and drained)
1 6-ounce jar artichoke hearts marinated in olive oil (chopped)
3 cups water
1 cup quinoa
1/2 cup frozen peas
1/2 cup frozen edamame
1/2 cup corn kernels
3 tablespoons olive oil
1 teaspoon cumin
1 teaspoon dried oregano
1 teaspoon dried basil
1/2 teaspoon sea salt
1/4 teaspoon ground
   black pepper
1/4 teaspoon dried cilantro
juice squeezed from 1 lime

Is it proper to put your pinky up when drinking tea?

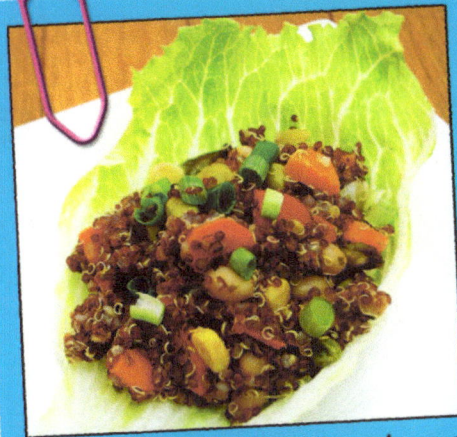

When someone says "mind your p's and q's," they mean to mind your manners and to behave.

RECIPE

Bring quinoa, water, and a pinch of salt to a boil in a saucepan. Reduce heat to medium-low, cover, and simmer until quinoa is tender, about 20 minutes. Once done, drain in a mesh strainer, and set aside.

Meanwhile, heat olive oil in a large skillet over medium heat. Stir in garlic, and cook until garlic softens, about 2 minutes. Add carrots and cook for 3-5 minutes, then add all vegetables (except green onions and beans) and edamame. Continue cooking until vegetables are soft, about 5-10 minutes. Add beans and cook for 2 more minutes. Season with salt, pepper, cumin, oregano, and basil, then cook for 1 additional minute. Stir in cooked quinoa and green onions. Add lime juice. Serve hot or cold.

Nutrition Content for One Serving:

Calories	Fat	Saturated Fat	Carbohydrates	Sodium	Sugars
151	7 g	1 g	19 g	252 mg	3 g

Melon Lip Smack n' Cheese

Level = ★★

ingredients:

2 cups whole grain elbow macaroni
2 cups cantaloupe (chopped)
1 cup heavy whipping cream
1 cup Parmesan cheese (grated)
¼ teaspoon salt
½ teaspoon ground black pepper

Thomas Jefferson introduced macaroni and cheese to the U.S. after eating it while visiting France.

Recipe created by

Chef Denise Perry

RECIPE

Cook macaroni according to package directions. In a saute pan over medium heat, add cantaloupe and stir frequently. Cantaloupe should eventually begin to soften and turn into juice-like consistency from heat.

Apply pressure with back of a spoon to help crush cantaloupe. Add heavy cream and bring to simmer. Add elbow macaroni evenly over mixture. Turn heat to low and sprinkle in parmesan cheese.

Stir well, and add salt and pepper.

Makes 8 servings.

Melon Mania

Can you name three types of melons? Some of the letters have been filled in to help you figure out the word!

1. w_t_r_e__n
2. _a_t_l_upe
3. __n_y_ew

Nutrition Content for One Serving:

Calories	Fat	Saturated Fat	Carbohydrates	Sodium	Sugars
263	15 g	7 g	29 g	317 mg	3 g

ANSWERS: 1. watermelon; 2. cantaloupe; 3. honeydew

Dinner Recipes:

Unscramble the words below and write the letter inside the boxes (with a number underneath) to reveal the answer to the question:

How many fruits and veggies should you eat a day?

NNABAA

PEAPL

WERTYBSARR ⁴

HYRCER ⁵

IWKI ¹

GOMNA

EYBLRUERB ²

SEAPGR ³

LEWATORNME

F	V		D		
1		2	3	4	5

Fish Boats

Level = ★★★

ingredients:

1 head of green cabbage OR
  6-8 whole cabbage leaves
2 limes (1 teaspoon juice and ½ teaspoon zest)
1 cup red onion (cut into thin strips)
1 red bell pepper (cut into thin strips)
1 teaspoon sea salt
1 bunch fresh cilantro (1 cup leaves with short stems)
1 pound fish fillets (like tilapia, mahi mahi, orata, or red snapper)
2 teaspoons olive oil
2 teaspoons garlic (minced)
¼ teaspoon ground black
  pepper
1 teaspoon ground cumin
1 teaspoon ground coriander
½ teaspoon paprika
½ teaspoon dried dill
¼ teaspoon crushed red
  pepper flakes
½ cup fat-free sour cream
½ cup fat-free mayonnaise
1 cup jicama (shredded)

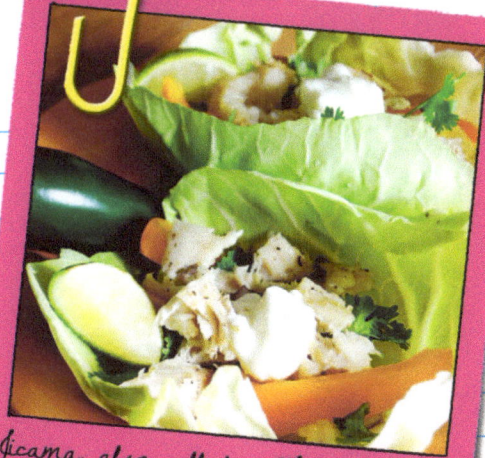

Jicama, also called a Mexican potato, looks like a big turnip and tastes like a potato when eaten raw.

salmon fillet

RECIPE

Preheat oven to 425°F. Peel and wash 6-8 largest cabbage leaves and pat dry. In bowl, mix together sour cream, mayonnaise, ½ teaspoon sea salt, and lime juice and zest; set aside. Clean fish fillets and dry with paper towel. Mix olive oil and garlic in small bowl; add ½ teaspoon salt, pepper, cumin, coriander, paprika, dill, and red pepper flakes. Place fish fillets in baking dish sprayed with non-stick cooking spray. Spread both fillet sides with spice and garlic mixture.

Bake 9 minutes or until fish flakes with a fork. Put fish in bowl; break into pieces with fork. Place a few pieces of cilantro, onion, red pepper and jicama in one cabbage leaf. Top with 1 tablespoon of fish and dollop of sour cream mixture. Serve with lime wedges. Makes 8 servings.

Nutrition Content for One Serving:

Calories	Fat	Saturated Fat	Carbohydrates	Sodium	Sugars
157	3 g	<1 g	16 g	193 mg	7 g

Curry in a Hurry Chicken
Level = ★★★

ingredients:
2 4-ounce boneless, skinless chicken breasts
4-ounce plain fat-free yogurt (use soy yogurt
   for lactose-free diet) OR 1/2 cup Greek yogurt
1/2 cup instant whole grain brown rice
1/2 cup yellow onion (chopped)
1/2 cup golden raisins
3 teaspoons no-salt-added tomato paste
2 teaspoons fat-free, low-sodium chicken broth
1 1/2 teaspoon curry powder
1 1/2 teaspoon dried cilantro
1 teaspoon lime juice
1/2 teaspoon minced garlic
1/4 teaspoon ground ginger

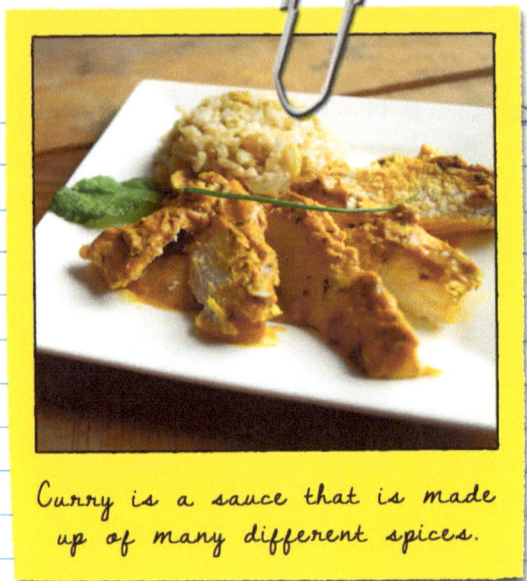

1/4 teaspoon salt
1/4 teaspoon ground black pepper
1/4 teaspoon ground turmeric

Curry is a sauce that is made up of many different spices.

Nutrition Content for One Serving:

Calories	Fat	Saturated Fat	Carbohydrates	Sodium	Sugars
240	1 g	<1 g	39 g	429 mg	17 g

Directions:

(1) Preheat oven to 375°F. Combine yogurt, 2 teaspoons of chicken broth, tomato paste, cilantro, lime juice, ginger, turmeric, and curry powder in shallow bowl. Put 2 tablespoons of sauce in a bowl, cover, and refrigerate.

(2) Salt and pepper each side of chicken. Place chicken in greased casserole dish and add yogurt sauce, coating evenly.

(3) Bake chicken, covered, for 35 minutes or until no longer pink in middle.

(4) While chicken is baking, bring 1/2 cup plus 2 tablespoons of water OR chicken broth to a boil in a saucepan over medium heat. Boil rice (covered) until tender (about 10 minutes), and most of liquid has absorbed. Stir in raisins, onion, and garlic and cook covered for 2-5 minutes. Turn off heat but keep covered until chicken is done.

(5) Spoon rice onto plate and top with chicken and yogurt (from fridge). Makes 4 servings.

Pork Stick 'em Up Kebabs

Level = ★★★

ingredients:

2 cloves garlic (finely minced)

1 8-ounce can pineapple chunks in 100% fruit juice (drain chunks but save ¼ cup of juice)

1½ pounds pork loin (lean, cut into 1-inch cubes)

1 orange bell pepper (cut into square chunks)

1 green bell pepper (cut into square chunks)

3 tablespoons low-sodium beef broth

1 package whole grain brown rice (cooked according to package instructions)

1 pint cherry tomatoes

2 medium carrots (sliced)

1 red onion (cut into chunks)

1 package whole button mushrooms (washed)

2 tablespoons low-sodium soy sauce

2 tablespoons red wine vinegar

1 tablespoon brown sugar

1 tablespoon canola oil

½ teaspoon ground ginger

½ teaspoon sea salt

¼ teaspoon dried basil

¼ teaspoon ground coriander

¼ teaspoon ground black pepper

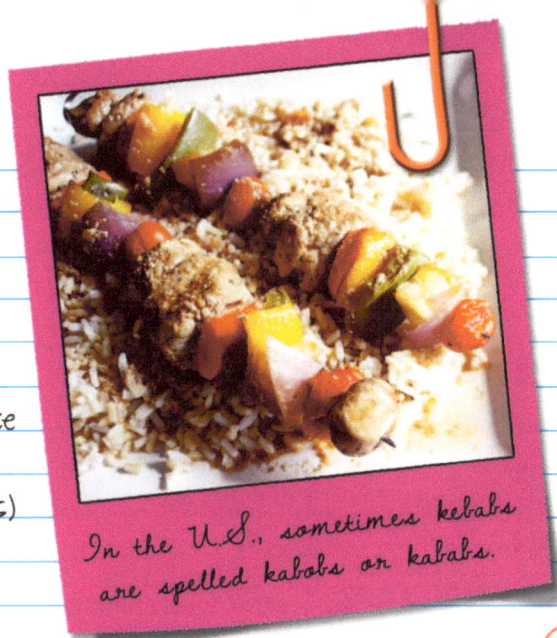

In the U.S., sometimes kebabs are spelled kabobs or kababs.

This is kebab written in Arabic! Did you know Arabic is read from right to left, the opposite of English?

كباب

RECIPE

In saucepan, bring 1 inch of water to boil, add carrots. Cover and cook for 10-12 minutes or until almost tender; drain well. Drain pineapple, but keep ¼ cup of juice. Set pineapple aside.

In bowl, combine vinegar, oil, soy sauce, salt, pepper, basil, coriander, broth, pineapple juice, brown sugar, garlic, and ginger with a wire whisk. Refrigerate 2 tablespoons of marinade for basting later. Place pork cubes in a 1-gallon plastic zip bag and pour in marinade; let stand for 30 minutes in refrigerator.

On metal or soaked wooden skewers, alternate pork, carrots, peppers, pineapple, onion, tomatoes, and mushrooms. Use chilled marinade to baste meat, then bake in oven on a cookie sheet at 400°F for 30 minutes or until meat is browned. Serve over rice.

Nutrition Content for One Serving:

Calories	Fat	Saturated Fat	Carbohydrates	Sodium	Sugars
245	8 g	3 g	25 g	603 mg	9 g

Chop Chop Chili
Level = ★★

page 34

chop chop means to do something quickly or in a hurry

ingredients:

2 16-ounce cans dark red kidney beans (drained)
1 16-ounce can light red kidney beans (drained)
1 15-ounce can no-salt-added corn
1 42-ounce can no-salt-added diced tomatoes
8 ounces fat-free shredded cheddar cheese
2 tablespoons chili powder
1½ cup zucchini (finely chopped)
1 cup carrots (finely chopped)
½ cup yellow squash (finely chopped)
½ cup red bell pepper (finely chopped)
½ cup celery (finely chopped)
¾ cup onion (chopped)
3 cloves garlic (minced)
1 teaspoon olive oil

½ teaspoon dried basil
½ teaspoon dried oregano
½ teaspoon ground cumin
½ teaspoon salt
¼ teaspoon ground black pepper

Add a dollop of sour cream for an extra taste boost!

60% of a kid's body is made up of water, so keep hydrated by drinking 5-8 glasses of water a day!

RECIPE

Rinse and drain both cans of beans. In a large pot, sauté onion, celery, and garlic in olive oil. Cook until soft. Add chili powder, basil, oregano, and cumin to onion and garlic; stir.

Stir in zucchini, squash, red bell pepper, and carrots, blend well. Cook 1-2 minutes over low heat, stirring occasionally. Add tomatoes, corn, and kidney beans. Bring to a boil. Reduce heat and simmer for 45 minutes or until thick. Add a pinch of cheese to each bowl before serving.

Makes 10 servings.

Nutrition Content for One Serving:

Calories	Fat	Saturated Fat	Carbohydrates	Sodium	Sugars
233	1 g	<1 g	39 g	547 mg	10 g

Buffalo Chicken Ziti

Level = ★★★

ingredients:

¼ teaspoon ground black pepper
1 teaspoon olive oil
1 teaspoon garlic (minced)
2 teaspoons hot sauce
1 tablespoon ranch dressing
4 tablespoons cream cheese
½ cup mozzarella cheese (shredded)
½ cup cheddar cheese (shredded)
1 cup frozen corn
1 cup celery (diced)
2 cups cooked shredded chicken (TIP: use store-bought rotisserie chicken!)
2 cups mini ziti pasta
2 cups tomatoes (diced)
¼ cup yellow onion (diced)

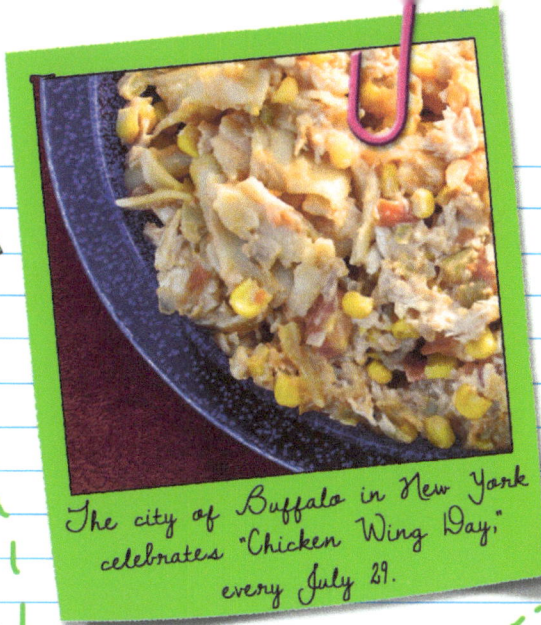

The city of Buffalo in New York celebrates "Chicken Wing Day," every July 29.

Buffalo chicken is an imposter! there's no buffalo in there!

Food for Thought:
Buffalo chicken has NO buffalo meat in it; it is all chicken. But because eating the wing part of the chicken started in Buffalo, New York, which explains its name!

RECIPE

Cook pasta until al dente according to package directions. Drain. Set aside. Heat oil in large skillet on medium heat. Add garlic and onion. Saute 1 minute. Add celery. Saute mixture until onions are translucent and celery is slightly soft, about 8 minutes. Add corn and tomatoes. Heat for 2 to 4 minutes or until tomatoes are just soft.

Add cream cheese. Stir until it is melted. Add ranch dressing and hot sauce. Stir to mix evenly. Add mozzarella and cheddar cheeses and stir until they are melted. Add chicken and pasta. Stir until thoroughly mixed. Serve hot. Makes 6 servings.

Nutrition Content for One Serving:

Calories	Fat	Saturated Fat	Carbohydrates	Sodium	Sugars
419	11 g	5 g	50 g	235 mg	5 g

Zesty Stir Fry

Level = ★★

好吃
hau chyr
means "yummy"

ingredients:

2 cups instant whole grain brown rice

1 pound boneless, skinless chicken breasts
   (thawed and cut into bite-sized pieces)

3 tablespoons low-sodium soy sauce

1 tablespoon sesame oil

½-1 tablespoon salt-free lemon pepper seasoning

1 14-ounce package mixed vegetables (thawed)

   OR 1¾ cups fresh vegetables of your choice (chopped)

Juice and zest of 1 large lemon

½ teaspoon sea salt

¼ cup honey

Zest is the leftover flavoring you get when you scrape or cut the outer skin of citrus fruits.

樂 ler (rhymes with near)
means "happiness"

炒

This Chinese word is chao (said just like chow), which is a way to prepare food in a wok pan. chao is a way to cook meat and vegetables quickly.

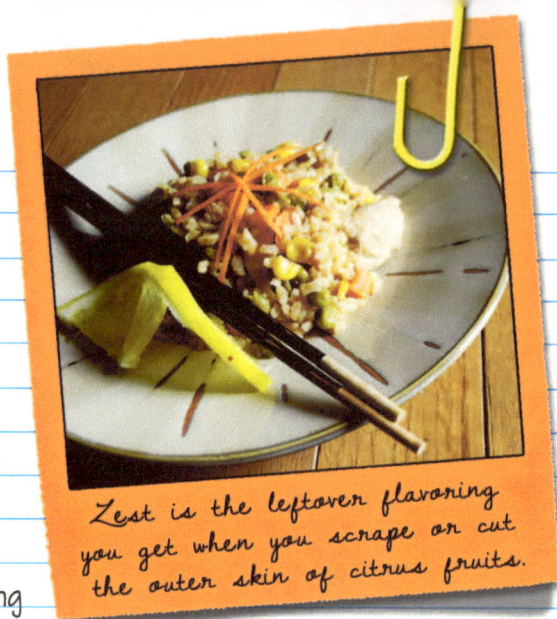

RECIPE

Prepare rice according to package directions.

Sprinkle chicken with lemon pepper and salt; then stir fry in oil for 10 minutes in large skillet or wok over medium-high heat. Mix soy sauce, honey, lemon juice, and zest in small bowl; blend well.

Combine cooked rice, sauce, and vegetables with chicken. Stir fry over high heat until heated through, about 2 minutes.

Makes 4 servings.

Nutrition Content for One Serving:

Calories	Fat	Saturated Fat	Carbohydrates	Sodium	Sugars
351	3 g	0 g	60 g	792 mg	17 g

Bean Me Up Burger

Level = ★★

ingredients:

1 egg

1 tablespoon garlic (chopped)

2 15-ounce cans black beans (rinsed and drained)

2 tablespoons cilantro leaves (chopped)

2 tablespoons parsley leaves (chopped)

½ medium yellow onion (finely chopped)

½ medium red bell pepper (finely chopped)

2 celery stalks (chopped)

2 carrot sticks (chopped)

¾ cup whole wheat bread crumbs

½ cup frozen corn kernels

¼ teaspoon ground black pepper

¼ teaspoon dried marjoram

½ teaspoon ground cumin

½ teaspoon lime juice

½ teaspoon salt

OPTIONAL: 1 teaspoon hot sauce

DO YOU KNOW WHICH SHOW WAS THE ONE THAT BECAME KNOWN FOR THE POPULAR SAYING: "BEAM ME UP SCOTTY"?

Black beans have the highest level of antioxidants of all beans, which can help prevent cancer.

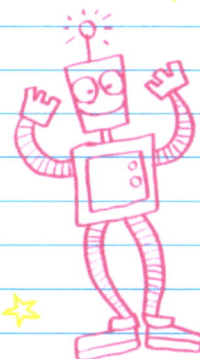

Question Answer: "Star Trek"

RECIPE

In food processor or blender, add carrots, celery, onion, garlic, red pepper, one can of black beans, cilantro, marjoram, parsley, egg, cumin, salt, pepper, lime juice, and hot sauce, and pulse until ingredients are mixed well (1-2 minutes).

Heat electric grill or grill pan over medium-low heat. Transfer mixture to mixing bowl, add other can of black beans, bread crumbs, and corn. Mix until combined. Divide mixture into portions and form into patties. Place patties on grill and cook about 6 minutes on each side, until heated through. Serve on whole grain hamburger bun with lettuce, tomato, and condiments.

Makes 6-8 burgers.

Nutrition Content for One Serving:

Calories	Fat	Saturated Fat	Carbohydrates	Sodium	Sugars
246	11 g	4 g	32 g	676 mg	14 g

Chicken Spice Rice

Level = ★★★

ingredients:

1 tablespoon olive oil
4 boneless, skinless chicken breasts (thawed)
1 medium green bell pepper (cut into ½-inch pieces)
¼ teaspoon ground black pepper
½ medium yellow onion (about ¼-¾ cup chopped)
1 tablespoon paprika
2 cloves garlic (crushed with garlic press)
1 14.5-ounce can no-salt-added diced tomatoes with juice
1 10-ounce package frozen peas
1¼ cups whole grain brown rice
½ cup green olives (diced)
1½ cups chicken broth or stock

1½ cups water
1 teaspoon dried cilantro
1 teaspoon dried oregano
½ teaspoon salt
¼ teaspoon chili powder

Piquant is another way to say that a food is hot as in spicy hot (think peppers and paprika!).

MORE YUMMY INGREDIENTS

instructions:

(1) Preheat oven to 350°F. In Dutch oven, heat oil on medium-high until hot. Sprinkle salt and pepper on chicken; cook, until lightly browned on both sides (about 6 minutes).

(2) With tongs, transfer chicken to small roasting pan or baking dish. Add ½ cup chicken stock or broth. Cover pan with foil and bake chicken until well done (25-30 minutes).

(3) Meanwhile, in same Dutch oven, cook green pepper, garlic, and onion about 10 minutes or until vegetables are tender, stirring occasionally. Stir in paprika, cilantro, oregano, and chili powder and cook 30 seconds. Add tomatoes with their juice, stock, water, and rice; heat to boiling on high.

(4) Reduce heat to low; cover and simmer 10 minutes. Stir in frozen peas and olives.

(5) Spoon rice mixture into greased baking dish. Transfer chicken into hot rice mixture. Cover and bake 25 minutes or until most of liquid is absorbed. Makes about 4-6 servings.

Nutrition Content for One Serving:					
Calories	Fat	Saturated Fat	Carbohydrates	Sodium	Sugars
282	7 g	<1 g	33 g	766 mg	7 g

Fintastic Fillet

Level = ★★

ingredients:

5-6 salmon fillets
12 basil leaves
3 green onions (cut into 1-inch sticks)
1 quart cherry tomatoes (cut in half)
1 tablespoon olive oil
2 large lemons
½ teaspoon sea salt
OPTIONAL: 1 bunch asparagus spears (cut into 1-inch segments)
¼ teaspoon ground
   black pepper

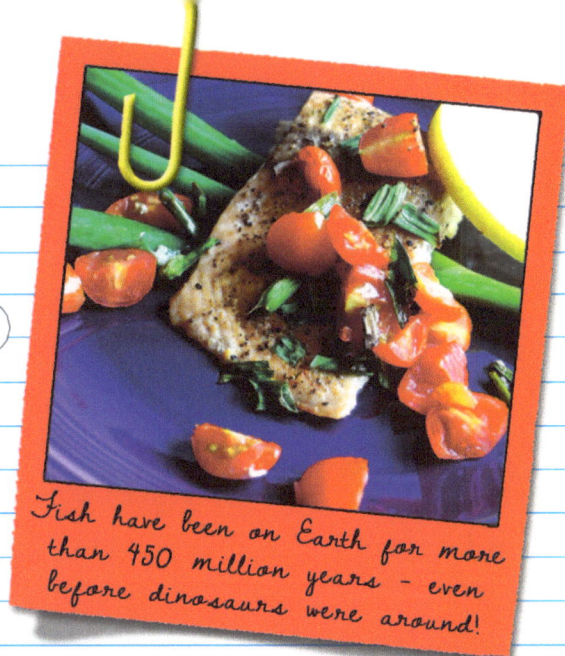

Fish have been on Earth for more than 450 million years - even before dinosaurs were around!

Seasoning Instructions

Mix together the following:
1 tablespoon dry mustard,
2 tablespoons celery salt,
1½ tablespoons ground
bay leaves, 1½ teaspoons
nutmeg, 1 teaspoon ground
cloves, 1 teaspoon ground
ginger, 1 teaspoon paprika,
and 1 teaspoon cayenne
pepper

RECIPE

Rinse and pat dry salmon fillets. Place salmon on parchment paper and season with few pinches of salt, pepper, and generous amount of seafood seasoning. Let salmon sit for 20 minutes to absorb seasonings.

Preheat oven to 400°F. Place salmon (skin skide down) on pan lined with parchment paper. Don't crowd fish. Place 1-2 basil leaves, green onions, chopped tomatoes, and asparagus (optional) on each fillet. Drizzle olive oil and squeeze lemon juice on each fillet.

Bake for about 15-22 minutes, depending on size of fillets. Check for doneness after 15-20 minutes. Makes 5-12 servings as fillets can be cut in half.

Nutrition Content for One Serving:

Calories	Fat	Saturated Fat	Carbohydrates	Sodium	Sugars
307	15 g	3 g	8 g	449 mg	4 g

Good Golly Gumbo

Level = ★★

ingredients:

2 slices bacon (cut into 1-inch pieces)
3 boneless, skinless chicken tenders (1-inch chunks)
1 pork steak (cut into 1-inch chunks)
  OR 1 pound ground pork sausage (cooked)
1 bunch asparagus spears (finely chopped)
2 14.5-ounce cans no-salt-added diced tomatoes
½ pound frozen or fresh shrimp (peeled, deveined, tails removed)
1 11.5-ounce can no-salt-added tomato juice
1 16-ounce package frozen corn
1 10-ounce package frozen okra
3 cups fat-free less-sodium chicken stock
2 cups whole grain brown rice
1 green bell pepper (seeded and chopped)
1 teaspoon dried thyme
¼ teaspoon hot sauce
2 bay leaves
1 teaspoon lemon juice
½ teaspoon salt
½ teaspoon dry mustard
½ teaspoon dried basil
¼ teaspoon dried parsley
¼ teaspoon paprika

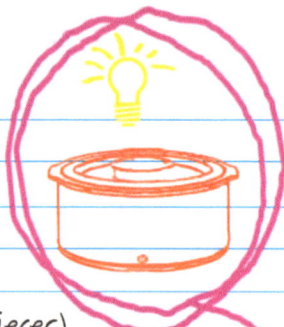

✓ 2 celery stalks (chopped)
✓ 1 cup yellow onion (chopped)
✓ 1 tablespoon garlic (minced)
✓ 1 teaspoon dried oregano
✓ ¼ teaspoon red pepper flakes
✓ ¼ teaspoon cayenne pepper
✓ ¼ teaspoon ground black pepper

Set on low, slow cookers run on the same amount of energy used to power a 100-watt light bulb!

RECIPE

Cook bacon in small skillet until almost crispy. Add cooked bacon to slow cooker. Add garlic, chicken, and pork. Add herbs and spices to meat and stir. Place vegetables in slow cooker and stir. Add tomato juice, tomatoes, chicken stock, lemon juice, and hot sauce and stir. Cover and place slow cooker on low for 6-8 hours or high for 3-4 hours. Add rice and shrimp to gumbo about 30 minutes before serving.

Makes 10 servings.

Nutrition Content for One Serving:

Calories	Fat	Saturated Fat	Carbohydrates	Sodium	Sugars
346	11 g	4 g	39 g	320 mg	8 g

Tuna Noodlerole

Level = ★★

ingredients:

2 6-ounce cans of tuna packed in water (drained)

3 tablespoons unsalted butter

1 small yellow onion (peeled and chopped)

2 tablespoons all-purpose flour

½ cup fat-free mozzarella cheese (shredded)

½ cup fat-free sharp OR mild cheddar cheese (shredded)

1 7.5-ounce jar artichoke hearts in oil (drained and chopped)

1½ cups cholesterol-free and 99%-fat-free whole wheat egg noodles

1½ teaspoons dried parsley

½ cup red bell pepper (chopped)

2 cups heavy cream

1 cup frozen peas

½ teaspoon sea salt

2 teaspoons garlic (minced)

½ teaspoon ground black pepper

OPTIONAL: ½ cup button mushrooms (chopped)

Tuna can swim up to 50 miles per hour – that's faster than a car driving in town!

RECIPE

Cook egg noodles with peas according to package directions; drain and set aside.

Melt unsalted butter in large, deep skillet and sauté onions (about 1/2 cup) and garlic over low heat until tender (about 2 minutes). Stir in flour to make thick paste. Add cream, salt, pepper, and parsley. Stir until flour is dissolved. Add red pepper and artichoke hearts (and mushrooms if desired). Cook and stir until bubbly and thickened. Add tuna, then stir in cheeses until melted.

Remove from heat and stir in noodles and peas until mixed well. Serve immediately. Makes 8 servings.

Nutrition Content for One Serving:

Calories	Fat	Saturated Fat	Carbohydrates	Sodium	Sugars
408	17 g	10 g	37 g	598 mg	4 g

Spaghetti Skillet

Level = **

ingredients:

6 ounces dried whole wheat spaghetti
½ pound lean ground turkey
¼ teaspoon ground black pepper
½ teaspoon Italian seasoning
2 tablespoons unsalted butter
½ cup yellow onion (chopped)
⅓ cup fat-free Parmesan cheese (grated)
1¼ cup natural spaghetti sauce (tomato and basil flavor is best)
1 cup fat-free cottage cheese (drained)
1 cup fat-free mozzarella cheese (shredded)
2 eggs (beaten)
¼ teaspoon salt

Did you know that October is National Pasta Month in the United States?

AL DENTE MEANS "TO THE TOOTH" IN ITALIAN, WHICH IS HOW TO TEST PASTA TO SEE IF THE NOODLE IS COOKED PROPERLY: IT SHOULD BE A BIT FIRM, BUT TENDER.

RECIPE

Cook spaghetti according to package directions and drain. Return spaghetti to warm saucepan. Toss with unsalted butter until it melts. Stir in Parmesan, ¾ cup mozzarella, and eggs. In skillet, cook ground turkey and onion until meat is brown. Drain off fat. Add salt, pepper, and Italian seasoning.

Coat 9-inch pie plate with non-stick cooking spray. Press spaghetti noodle mixture onto bottom and up sides of plate to form a crust. Spoon cottage cheese onto crust.

Stir spaghetti sauce into browned meat. Spoon over cottage cheese. Sprinkle with rest of mozzarella. Bake at 350°F oven for 20-25 minutes, or until bubbly.

Nutrition Content for One Serving:

Calories	Fat	Saturated Fat	Carbohydrates	Sodium	Sugars
343	12 g	4 g	35 g	648 mg	8 g

Party Treats & Snack Recipes:

Fitness Fun Crossword

Work off those extra calories and earn those yummy party treats and desserts by exercising! See if you can figure out fun fitness activities from the clues below.

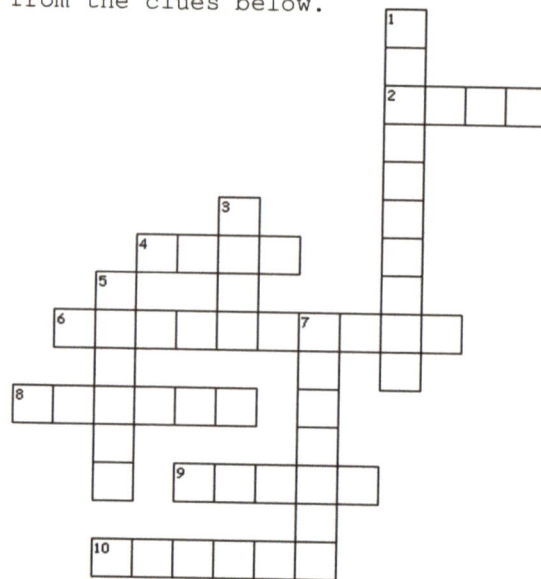

Across:
2. What you do with a jumprope
4. Activity you do in a pool
6. Sport in which you use your hands to knock a ball over the net to other side
8. Sport in which you use stick to hit a puck
9. Moving to beat of music
10. Activity in which you use self-discipline and control to kick and punch

Down:
1. Sport in which you throw a ball through a hoop
3. To walk outdoors in nature
5. Sport in which you kick a goal
7. Pedal this for good exercise

Across Answers: (2) skip; (4) swim; (6) volleyball; (8) hockey; (9) dance; (10) karate
Down Answers: (1) basketball; (3) hike; (5) soccer; (7) bicycle

Luau Sorbet

Level = ★

ingredients:

1 10-ounce can pineapple in 100% fruit juice (drained)
1 10-ounce can grapefruit chunks in light syrup (drained)
1 11-ounce can mandarin oranges (drained)
2 cups 100% pure pulp-free orange juice
½ cup water
½ cup sugar
1 tablespoon lemon juice
2 teaspoons freshly grated orange zest
2 teaspoons freshly grated lemon zest

Only 1 blossom out of 100 becomes a "grown" orange fruit - so that means 99 others don't make the cut!

A luau is a Hawaiian party with a BIG feast and LOTS of entertainment!

Nutrition Content for One Serving:

Calories	Fat	Saturated Fat	Carbohydrates	Sodium	Sugars
92	<1g	0 g	23 g	8 mg	21 g

RECIPE

In medium saucepan, bring water and sugar to a boil. Let cool.

Combine sugar water, pineapple, grapefruit, and mandarin oranges in food processor and blend until smooth. Transfer mixture to metal bowl and stir in lemon juice, orange juice, lemon zest, and orange zest. Freeze until slightly firm (about 1-2 hours), but not frozen.

Beat mixture again in food processor or beat with an electric mixer until smooth. Transfer to a freezer container and freeze until firm, about 2 hours.

Makes 12 servings.

The pineapple is a symbol for hospitality and to welcome strangers. This goes back to the time when people in the West Indies and the early Americas would place pineapples at the village entrance to welcome visitors!

Sassy Salsa

Level = *

ingredients:

1½ cups red and yellow tomatoes
1 tablespoon green chiles (diced)
½ cup onion (chopped)
1½ teaspoons lime juice
1 teaspoon garlic (minced)
½ teaspoon salt
¼ teaspoon ground black pepper
¼ teaspoon ground coriander
¼ teaspoon dried cilantro

Salsa means sauce in Spanish. Now, more people in America add salsa instead of ketchup to meals!

RECIPE

Stir all ingredients together in a medium bowl with a big spoon.

To make it a little spicier, add ¼ teaspoon chili powder.

For milder salsa, don't include the green chiles.

Serve with whole wheat or low-fat tortilla chips.

Makes 6 servings.

1.
2.
3.
4.
5.

Answers: (1) peanut butter; (2) jelly or jam; (3) mustard; (4) ketchup; (5) pepper

Definition: condiment

kŏn'də-mənt (**noun**)
- A type of dressing or sauce used to add flavor to food (like salsa).

Can you name the five types of condiments drawn above? Write the name next to the correct number below:

1.
2.
3.
4.
5.

Nutrition Content for One Serving (Salsa Only; Does Not Include Chips):

Calories	Fat	Saturated Fat	Carbohydrates	Sodium	Sugars
17	<1 g	<1 g	4 g	208 mg	2 g

Jumping Jacks Bean Dip
Level = ★

ingredients:

1 medium garlic bulb
2 teaspoons olive OR canola oil
3 tablespoons lemon juice
1 teaspoon dried parsley
1 teaspoon dried rosemary
1 teaspoon ground sage
1/4 teaspoon salt
1/4 teaspoon ground black pepper
1 15.5-ounce can great northern beans (drained; keep 2 tablespoons of liquid)

The myth that garlic wards away vampires symbolizes using it to prevent mosquitoes from biting!

Nutrition Content for One Serving:

Calories	Fat	Saturated Fat	Carbohydrates	Sodium	Sugars
56	1g	<1 g	10 g	347 mg	4 g

RECIPE

Place all ingredients in a food processor, cover, and puree until mixture is creamy and thick.

Spoon dip into a serving dish and sprinkle with parsley.

Serve with raw vegetables, pita bread quarters, or pita chips.

Makes 8 servings.

Uncle Tong likes doing jumping jacks to exercise. He burns 5 calories for every minute that he does jumping jacks.

If Uncle Tong wanted to burn 50 calories, how many minutes would he have to do jumping jacks?

5 calories	50 calories
1 minute	____ minutes

Hint: multiply 50 calories x 1 minute and divide by 5 calories

Easy Cheesy Quiche Bites

Level = ★★

ingredients

1 egg

1 tomato (diced small and patted dry with a paper towel)

3 tablespoons heavy whipping cream

4 asparagus spears (cut crosswise into ¼-inch-thick pieces)

½ cup Gruyere or Swiss cheese (shredded)

¼ cup yellow onion (very finely chopped)

1 package puff pastry dough sheet (found in frozen section of grocery store)

½ teaspoon ground black pepper

½ teaspoon garlic (minced)

½ teaspoon salt

¼ teaspoon dried dill

¼ teaspoon dried basil

Quiche is the savory opposite of pie and has savory insides rather than sweet ingredients.

Definition:
savory

sā-v-rē (adjective)

- very flavorful type of food that offers a pleasant taste; opposite of sweet type of food
- examples: cheese, meat, vegetables, spices

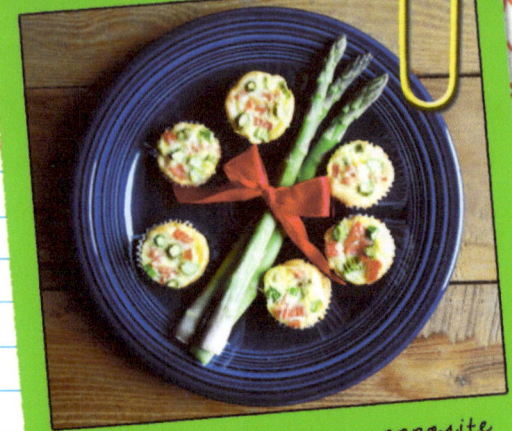

RECIPE

Preheat oven to 375°F. Unroll dough until flat and cut into 12 equal squares.

Line mini muffin tins with mini paper baking cups. Place dough squares in cups and shape edges to keep contents from spilling out. Divide cheese among cups; top with vegetables. Pat down with a spoon.

In a small bowl, combine egg and whipping cream and beat until frothy. Add garlic, salt, pepper, dill, basil, and stir.

Spoon egg mixture over vegetable filling to edge of tin. Bake for about 15 minutes. Cool before serving. Makes 12 servings.

Nutrition Content for One Serving:

Calories	Fat	Saturated Fat	Carbohydrates	Sodium	Sugars
75	6 g	3 g	3 g	209 mg	1 g

Fruit Skewers

Level = ★

A foot is 12 inches - so if you had a skewer that was half of a foot, how many inches is it?

ingredients:

1 kiwi (skin removed, cut in half, sliced thick)

1 1/2 pints fresh strawberries (stems removed)

1/2 cup green seedless grapes

1/2 cup red seedless grapes

1/2 cup fat-free plain or vanilla yogurt

2 tablespoons agave nectar

1/2 teaspoon lime zest

1 11-ounce can pineapple chunks in 100% fruit juice (drained)

4-6 bamboo skewers (cut in half)

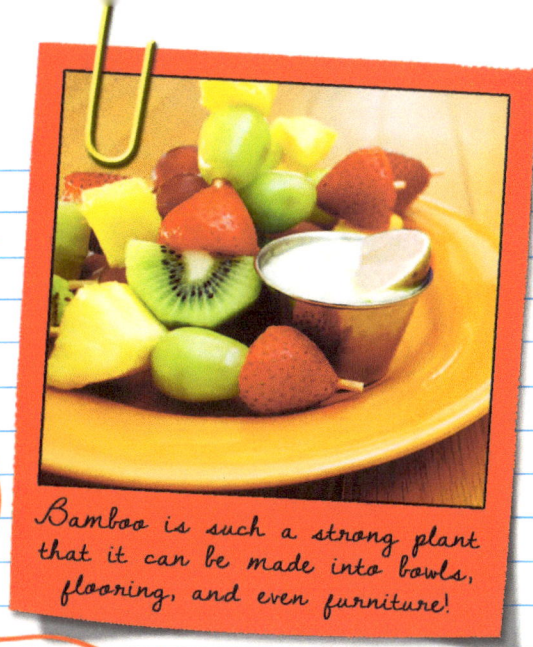

Bamboo is such a strong plant that it can be made into bowls, flooring, and even furniture!

Answer: 6 inches

Nutrition Content for One Skewer:

Calories	Fat	Saturated Fat	Carbohydrates	Sodium	Sugars
76	<1 g	<1 g	19 g	13 mg	16 g

what do you call 3 strawberries playing in a musical band?

strawberry jam!

RECIPE

To make this recipe, you can use fruits listed in ingredients, any fruit that is in season, or your favorite fruits. Nectarines, bananas, and mangoes are also great! Wash and dry fruit. Set aside.

In small bowl, combine yogurt, lime zest, and agave nectar for dipping sauce. Mix well.

Thread fruit onto skewers, alternating different fruits. Serve with dipping sauce. Refrigerate extra sauce in an airtight container.

Makes 8 or more fruit skewers (depending on size and amount of fruit used).

Good to Go Bars

Level = ⭐⭐

ingredients:

3 cups whole grain cereal

½ cup old fashioned OR quick cooking oats

½ cup honey

¼ cup pecans (chopped)

¼ cup dry roasted sunflower seeds

¼ cup golden raisins

¼ cup unsalted butter

¼ cup pitted dates (chopped)

1½ cups sugar-free dried apples (chopped) or 1½ cups Gala apples (peeled and diced)

⅓ cup no-sugar-added natural peanut butter, chunky or smooth (your preference)

1 tablespoon packed brown sugar

½ teaspoon ground cinnamon

The Granny Smith apple gets its name from its founder, Mrs. Mary Ann (Granny) Smith.

Nutrition Content for One Serving:

Calories	Fat	Saturated Fat	Carbohydrates	Sodium	Sugars
232	8 g	1 g	40 g	4 mg	16 g

Recipe Instructions:

(1) Line bottom and sides of 8-inch square pan with foil; spray foil with cooking spray. Sprinkle ½ cup of the apples over bottom of pan. Place cereal in resealable food storage plastic bag; seal bag and coarsely crush with rolling pin or meat mallet. Set aside.

(2) In a 4-quart Dutch oven, heat ½ cup of the apples, honey, raisins, dates, and brown sugar to boiling over medium-high heat, stirring occasionally. Reduce heat to medium. Cook uncovered about 1 minute, stirring constantly until hot and bubbly. Remove from heat.

(3) Stir peanut butter into cooked mixture until melted. Stir in butter, cinnamon, oats, and sunflower seeds until well mixed. Stir in crushed cereal.

(4) Press mixture very firmly and evenly onto apples in pan. Sprinkle remaining apples and pecans over mixture; press lightly into bars. Refrigerate about 2 hours or until set. Cut into 12 bars. Store covered in refrigerator.

Sugar & Spice Popcorn

Level = ★

ingredients:

3 cups plain microwave popcorn
2 tablespoons sugar
½ teaspoon ground cinnamon
¼ teaspoon ground nutmeg

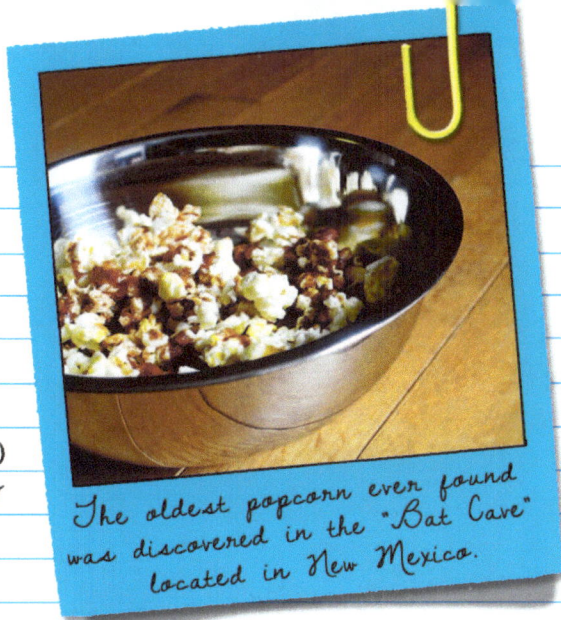

The oldest popcorn ever found was discovered in the "Bat Cave" located in New Mexico.

Nutrition Content for One Serving:

Calories	Fat	Saturated Fat	Carbohydrates	Sodium	Sugars
27	2 g	<1 g	4 g	45 mg	<1 g

RECIPE

Prepare popcorn according to package instructions.

Place hot popcorn in large bowl and spray with non-stick cooking spray. Add sugar and spices.

Toss gently until everything is mixed well.

Makes 4 servings.

Did You Know?

Popcorn is one of the oldest snacks - Native American Indians popped corn over campfires almost 5,000 years ago! Popcorn is thought to have originally come from Mexico, but is now eaten all around the world!

Cheesecake Cups

Level = ★★

ingredients:

2 ounces fat-free cream cheese
1¾ cups cold fat-free milk
½ cup frozen fat-free whipped topping (thawed)
1 ounce package of instant lemon pudding
1 teaspoon grated lemon zest
¼ teaspoon real vanilla extract
¾ cup fresh or frozen unsweetened blackberries (thawed)
1½ cup fresh or frozen unsweetened mixed berries (thawed)
8 reduced-fat vanilla wafer cookies OR 8 reduced-fat shortbread variety cookies (crumbled)
1½ tablespoons honey

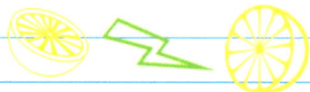

Parfait means "perfect" in French and usually refers to perfectly layered dessert treats.

How To ZEST a Citrus:

1. Hold fruit in one hand. With other hand, remove colored portion of peel by scraping with a fork or zesting tool.
2. Or for fine pieces, grate peel with a grater.
3. To make strips, use a vegetable peeler.

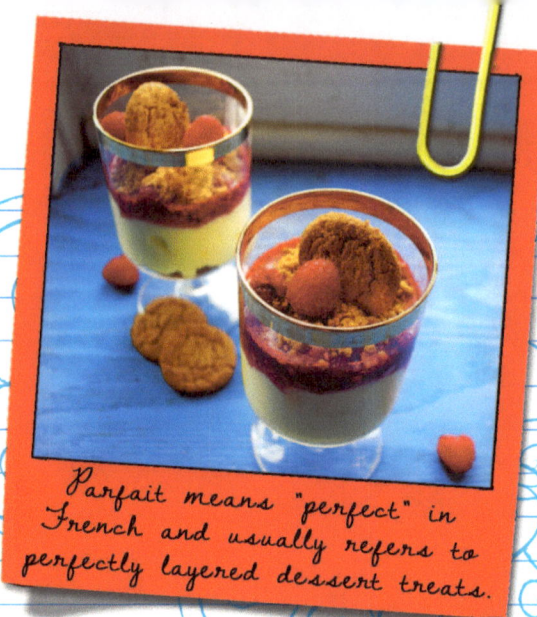

RECIPE

Sprinkle a thin layer of crumbled cookies into four dessert cups, reserving a small amount of cookie crumbles for the top of each cup at the end.

In a medium bowl, beat lemon pudding and milk with a mixer until pudding powder is dissolved. Add cream cheese, whipped topping, and lemon zest and blend with a mixer until smooth. Divide between the four dessert cups on top of the cookie crumbles. Then refrigerate for 1 hour.

In a small bowl, stir together mixed berries, honey, and vanilla. When gelatin is firm, top each serving with the berry mixture and sprinkle with the remaining cookie crumbles. Makes 4 servings.

Nutrition Content for One Serving:

Calories	Fat	Saturated Fat	Carbohydrates	Sodium	Sugars
141	2 g	<1 g	26 g	194 mg	14 g

All But the Kitchen Sink Cookies

Level = ★★

ingredients:

1 teaspoon real vanilla extract

2 eggs

1 cup firmly packed brown sugar

½ pound (2 sticks) unsalted butter (softened)

2 cups quick cooking or old fashioned oats (uncooked)

1 cup no-sugar-added natural chunky unsalted peanut butter

½ cup plus 2 tablespoons whole wheat flour

½ cup granulated sugar

½ cup plus 2 tablespoons all-purpose flour

½ cup dark chocolate chips

1 teaspoon baking soda

1 teaspoon baking powder

1 teaspoon ground cinnamon

¼ teaspoon salt

OPTIONAL: ½ cup walnuts

OPTIONAL: ½ cup raisins

Dark chocolate has a lot of antioxidants, which chew up bad elements that cause heart disease.

The saying, "All but the kitchen sink" is an idiom which means almost all that you can imagine is inside or included, which is perfect for the ingredients in this recipe! Yum!

RECIPE

Preheat oven to 350°F. Mix oats, both kinds of flour, baking soda, baking powder, cinnamon, and salt in a small bowl. In a large bowl, use an electric mixer to beat together unsalted butter and both sugars on medium speed. Beat in eggs and vanilla. Add flour mixture until well blended. Stir in peanut butter, chocolate chips, and walnuts and raisins (if desired).

Drop round spoonfuls at least 2 inches apart on a cookie sheet that has been lightly sprayed with non-stick cooking spray. Bake 11-20 minutes or until golden brown.

Makes approximately 24 cookies.

Nutrition Content for One Serving:

Calories	Fat	Saturated Fat	Carbohydrates	Sodium	Sugars
235	14 g	6 g	24g	131 mg	15 g

Squish Squash Sweet Fries

Level = ★★

ingredients:
1 or 2 large sweet potatoes
1 medium unsalted butternut squash
2 tablespoons seasoning salt

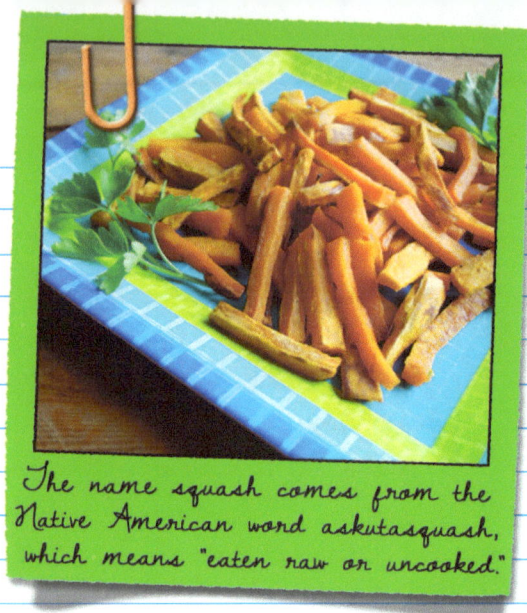

Can you name the foods, like French fry,
that start with the word "French?"
1. French t _ _ s _
2. French _ ni _ n s
3. French d _ _ s s _ n _
4. French _ i p
5. French b _ e _ d

Seasoning Variations:

For sweet fries, season with:
– 1 teaspoon brown sugar
– ¼ teaspoon ground cinnamon
– ¼ teaspoon ground nutmeg

For savory fries, season with:
– ¼ cup grated parmesan cheese
– ¼ teaspoon dried rosemary
– ¼ teaspoon dried thyme
– ¼ teaspoon dried oregano

The name squash comes from the Native American word askutasquash, which means "eaten raw or uncooked."

RECIPE

Preheat oven to 425°F. Remove ends of squash, peel with a vegetable peeler, cut in half lengthwise, and scoop out all seeds. Peel sweet potatoes using vegetable peeler, cut in half lengthwise, and then cut in half again. Cut squash and sweet potatoes into French fry shape. Soak up extra moisture with a paper towel.

Place all fries in a bowl and lightly spray nonstick cooking spray. Add seasoning salt and use hands to toss evenly. Add any other seasonings at this time. Transfer to cookie sheet or baking pan sprayed with nonstick cooking spray. Bake for 40 minutes, and flip halfway through baking. Makes 10-12 servings.

Answers: (1) French toast; (2) French onions; (3) French dressing; (4) French dip; (5) French bread

Nutrition Content for One Serving:

Calories	Fat	Saturated Fat	Carbohydrates	Sodium	Sugars
17	<1 g	<1 g	4 g	386 mg	<1 g

Healthy Tips, Tidbits & Techniques

Can you help Freddy Fork and Cousin Spatula to escape from the Junk Food Monster in Junk Food Hollow and safely get to Veggie Castle?

Tips, Tricks & Tidbits

Turn the handles of pots and pans that are on the stove in so that you don't accidentally bump into them and cause hot stuff to spill on you.

Rinse all fruits and vegetables under clean running water before cooking or eating.

ALWAYS keep hot foods HOT and cold foods COLD whether you're cooking or eating.

Don't lick your fingers or put your hands in your mouth when you work with raw foods, like cookie dough and meat.

You can eat your favorite snack or treat, but be food-friendly and share with someone else to enjoy it without overdoing it!

Be a Food Adventurer: Try lots of different types and colors of foods because you never know - even foods that are gross-looking can be very delicious-tasting!

KEEP OVEN MITTS OUT AND EASY TO GRAB WHEN YOU'RE COOKING OR BAKING.

Think healthy for your body and the environment:
- use fabric reusable bags instead of plastic bags when you go to the grocery store
- recycle plastic bottles, aluminum cans, and glass jars
- grow your own garden to replace what you've taken from the earth.

Kitchen Tools

Blender

Spatula

Oven Mitt

Wooden Spoon

Grater

Skillet/Frying Pan
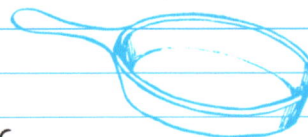

Rolling Pin

Whisk

Peeler

Electric Mixer

Cutting Board
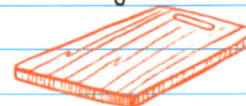

Colander

Masher

Scale

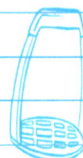

Casserole Dish
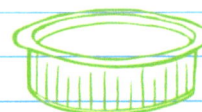

Dry Measuring Cups

Mixing Bowl

Can Opener
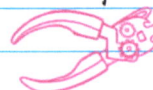

Liquid Measuring Cup

Measuring Spoons

Ladle

Dutch Oven

Chef Cheat Sheet: Terms A Cook Should Know

Blend To mix something evenly

Diced tomatoes

Brown To cook or bake a food until it turns a darker, or brown shade

Chop To cut up food into pieces that aren't exactly the same size

Cube To cut food up into square-like shapes

You don't have to wear a hat, but be sure to tie your hair back if it's long

Dice To cut a piece into cubes smaller than 1/2 inch

Drain To remove all of the liquid from food

You can use a colander to drain food.

Grease To spray or coat a pan or dish with butter, margarine, or olive oil so food doesn't stick to the pan or dish

Marinate To soak food in a liquid mixture of spices, oil, and/or vinegar so it absorbs the flavor; usually you marinate meat

Mince The smallest size you can cut a food; you mince garlic, herbs, and ginger; think the size of onions usually on a hamburger from a fast food joint

Preheat To warm up the oven before baking something

Sauté To cook food with oil or butter in a shallow pan over high heat

Simmer To heat a liquid so that it is close to a boil, but not hot enough to create bubbles

Whip To mix ingredients quickly and thoroughly, usually done with light foods or liquids like eggs or cream

Use a whisk to whip!

Fitness Fun!

Children need at least 60 minutes of physical activity a day.

Exercise can help fight off disease. It can slow or help prevent heart disease, stroke, high blood pressure, high cholesterol, type 2 diabetes, arthritis, osteoporosis, and loss of muscle mass.

Take a bike ride and take turns being the leader. After 15 minutes, stop to have some water, then try to find the longest way home!

Give each member of your family a pedometer (a device you wear to count how many steps you take) and have a competition to see who walks the most steps in a day, in a week, and then in a month. You can buy an inexpensive pedometer at most dollar stores.

Studies show that the more physically active a child is, the less she/he gets in trouble at school and the better her/his grades are.

Exercise makes your heart stronger. Your heart is the most important muscle in your body so the best way to be sure to grow strong and healthy is to exercise as much as you can and as often as you can!

Make a rule in your family that every time someone talks on the phone, he or she has to walk during the whole conversation. For motor mouths, this could add up to <u>lots</u> of miles per year!

To earn your 60 minutes of exercise each day, you don't have to do it all at once! You can exercise in 10-minute chunks throughout the day. No matter how may times you exercise or for how long each time, you're increasing your metabolism!

Plant a garden with your family. Not only is planting a great workout, so is tending the garden and picking the crops.

Plan a mini-Olympics with your friends, family, and neighbors! Design your own courses and competitions like who can do the most push-ups, who can jump rope the most times, who can run the fastest, and other fun and fit events. Together, come up with medals to award to winners and participants!

These Fitness Fun tips were provided by Kimberly Flanagan, M.S. Ed., former Physical Activity Action Team Leader for gen≠kids in Springfield, Illinois.

Glossary

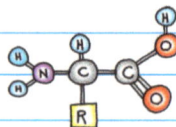

Amino acid: protein building blocks in the body

Antioxidant: a handful of nutrients and other substances that may slow the aging process, and also lower the risk of infections and some cancers

Calcium: mineral needed for healthy bones and teeth

Calorie: a measure of energy that food supplies to the body

Carbohydrates: a part of food that the body needs for energy; fruits, vegetables, milk, and grains are foods that contain carbohydrates

Cholesterol: a fatty substance found in the body and also in certain foods, such as meat and eggs; too much cholesterol in the body can clog blood flow to and from your heart

Diabetes: a disease which causes a person's pancreas to make little or no insulin to help move glucose out of the blood to give energy to the rest of the body

Enzyme: protein that causes reactions in the body, like digesting food

Fat: an oily substance that provides flavor to food; some fats are healthy (unsaturated) and some fats are unhealthy (saturated and trans fats); avoid eating too much fat

Fiber: a part of food that cannot be digested by the body, but has been proven to reduce blood sugar and lowers high cholesterol; fiber has been proven to reduce the risk of cancer

Fructose: sugar that is naturally found in fruit and honey and used to sweeten some food

Glucose: main type of sugar made in the body after eating food; glucose is needed to give energy and fuel to the body

Gluten: a type of protein found in flour and many other foods; people diagnosed with Celiac Disease are allergic to gluten and must eat a gluten-free diet

Glycemic Index: a measure of how foods affect glucose levels in the blood; if a food has a high GI, it causes glucose levels to raise blood sugar quicker than those that have a low GI

Mineral: a nutrient the body needs to work properly and is found in food and/or medicine

Nutrient: type of substance needed for energy and growth in people, animals and plants; carbohydrates, protein, and fat are examples of nutrients

Obese: a person who is obese has too much body fat and is at risk to develop diseases and/or serious health problems like heart disease (which can lead to heart attacks or strokes), diabetes, and high blood pressure; it can be calculated by Body Mass Index based on height and weight

Glossary - continued

Organic: a term used when food is grown using only natural animal or vegetable fertilizers and without the use of chemical sprays or insecticides

Portion: a serving size or amount of food

Poultry: term used to describe chickens, turkeys, ducks, or geese

Protein: the body-building nutrient provided by foods like milk, meat, cheese, and beans

Starch: a white, tasteless carbohydrate found in potatoes, grains, and other vegetables

Vegan: a person who doesn't eat/drink foods that come from animals, such as meat, fish, poultry, eggs, milk, and cheese

Vegetarian: a person who eats and drinks foods only made from plants (no meat or food made from animals) like grains, beans, nuts, vegetables, and fruits

Vitamin: very important substances found in food that your body needs to stay healthy and to function properly; below is a list of what job each vitamin performs:

- **Vitamin A:** keeps your skin and your eyes healthy; found in foods like carrots
- **Vitamin B:** a team of vitamins found in leafy green vegetables that help your body make protein and energy
- **Vitamin C:** helps your body to fight against infections and to heal faster, protect healthy gums, and to absorb (use) iron; found in foods like oranges
- **Vitamin D:** found in foods like milk, this vitamin makes your bones and teeth strong
- **Vitamin E:** lowers risk of heart disease, stroke, and certain cancers

Whole grains: foods made from the entire grain kernel which provide fiber and many more nutrients than white flour, which is used to make white bread and pasta

The glossary was compiled from a variety of research and information sources including:
- Sara Lopinksi, RD, BS, MS - Registered Dietitian at SIU School of Medicine
- WWW.KIDSHEALTH.ORG
- WWW.KIDS.JDRF.ORG

Measurement Mania

Measurement Key

1 tablespoon (tbsp.) =	½ cup =	1 gallon =
1 teaspoon (tsp.) =	⅓ cup =	1 quart =
1 cup =	¼ cup =	1 ounce =

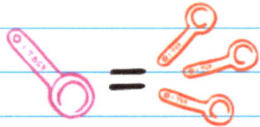

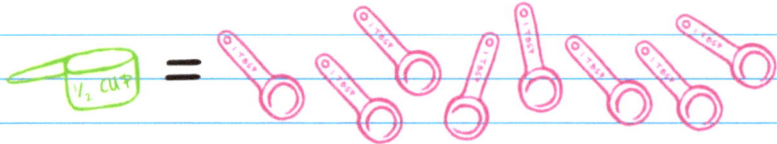

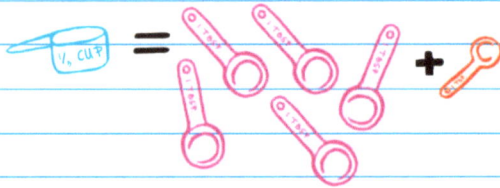

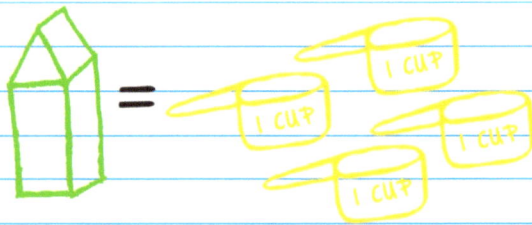

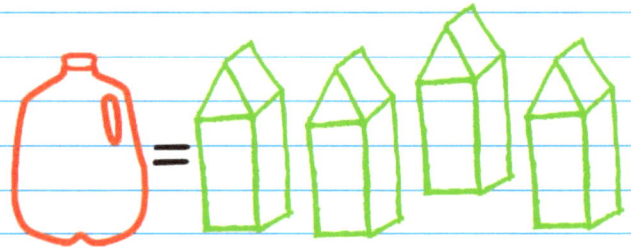

16 ounces = 1 pound

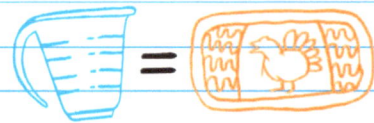

Freddy, Fork it Over! Family & Friends

THANK YOU to the amazing people and organizations listed below who helped Brandy and Farah to bring Freddy Silverton, his family, his recipes, and his healthy living tips to life -- and to help all kids make better choices!

Alex Herter
Alexis Deweese
Amanda Eichholz
Amanda Vinicky
Andrew Bodewes
Angie Shook Satchivi
Ann Gemberling
Ann Schmitt
Annie Wheeler
Anthony Lowder
April Hawes
Ashlyn Horcharik
Ayla Satchivi
Barbara Rowe
Barbara Salim
Becky Rader
Black Willow Photography
Blake Stadel
Bob Parrish
Brandy Moore Grove
Brian Reardon
Buffi Kaufman
Buffy Pennell
Cathy Spenseberger
Christina Gottemoller
Christina Robinson-Race
Christie Hovey
Claire Bitner
Connie Dilley
Cora Esela
Courtney Comeaux
Courtney Halford
Courtney Smith
Daniel Eck
Danielle Costello
Dave Daniels
Debby Bitner
Delaney Gortney
Denise Perry
Diana DeWeese
Dina Michaels
Dutch Grove
Erica Christell
Eva Svedberg Blomqvist
Farah Salim Eck
Fritz Goebig
Gary Moore
Geri Binkin
Holly Dahlquist
Izzy Grove
Jack McLaughlin
Jackie Campos
Jake Lieberman
Jay Kitterman
Jen Deaner
Jennifer Hoerner
Jennifer Jennings
Jenny Owens
Jerissa McCracken
Jerry Calbow

Jessica Dalheim
Jessica McGee
Jill Schuller
Jody Jacobs
Joe Langfelder
John Stephen Grove
Judy Horcharik
Julie Herter
Julie Waldrop
Kaitlyn Miller
Kara Wagner
Karen Hasara
Karen Kloppe
Karen Wagner
Kassidy Snyder
Kate Cohorst
Kathy Dehen
Kathy Wheeler
Kelli Kauffman-Bruns
Kemia Sarraf, MD, MPH
Kim Little
Kimberly Eck
Kimberly Flanagan
Kimberly Luz
Kimberly Smoot
Kristin Wagner
Kristina Mucinskas
Kristina Rasmussen
Kristy Gilmore
Kyleigh James
Laura Nestler
Lauren Davis
Leslie Cully
Leslie McConnell
Lincoln Grove
Linda Anderson
Lisa Corea
Lou Ann Moore
Lynette Nelson
Lynne Lowder
Madison Lieberman
Maria Lowder
Marilyn Raney
Mark Cully
Marque Haupert
Mary Rogers
Melanie Downs
Melanie Stivers
Melissa Hansen
Melissa Skinner-Liberman
Melissa Thompson
Merle Shiffman
Michael Camacho
Michael Eck
Michelle Villere
Mike Chrisman
Miranda Singler
Morgan Manning
Myrna Golay
Natalie McLaughlin

Noel Daniels
Olivia Bohringer
Paulette Dove
Rebecca Brown
Rebecca Sparks Korossy
Rick Lowder
Rita Calbow
Roberto Campos
Sandy Rutherford
Sara Lopinski, RD, BS, MS
Sara Ratcliffe
Sarah McLaughlin
Sarah Riopell
Stacey Brown
Stephanie Berry
Stephanie Moy-Zobus
Sue Nelson
Tina Grove
Tina Lieberman
Tony Bianco
Vanessa Little
Vanessa Parrish

Super Duper Supporters

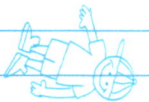

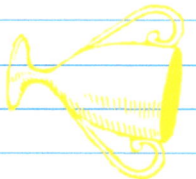

Index

The listing below breaks down the recipe pages into categories by main ingredient or type of food. So find a page below using ingredients you already have in your kitchen, or plan to make something new to taste! You never know what you'll love until you try it!

* vegetarian recipes listed above include eggs

SQUARE OFF - With a friend, take turns drawing a straight line from each dot, and whoever makes the last square wins!

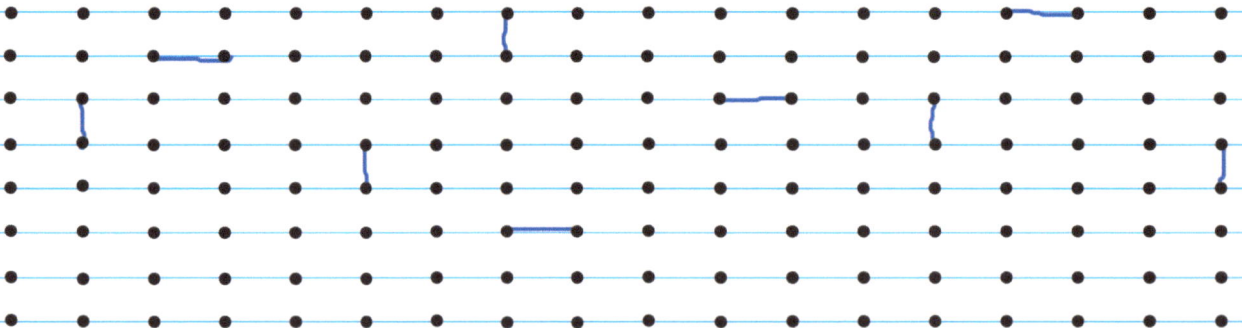